T0270032

Praise for Brian Propp
and *Angel on My Wing*

"[Brian Propp's comeback] is truly remarkable. You call on a lot of the reserves that you have as a professional athlete. He lasted a long time as a player, he had great resiliency as a player, and that's what you call on when you're confronted with situations like this. [His comeback] is great to see. You have to be fortunate along the way, but to come back fully from that is amazing.

I would have to believe that his strong faith played into his recovery. The power of the mind is a great thing. There are a lot of people in the sport we played that had talent, but the separators were the guys who could also put the thought perspective into play. If 'Propper' were to believe that, that's a huge part of the positive aspect of that, it's a huge factor.

The Chelios incident [elbowing Propp into the boards, rendering him unconscious]—those are just such scary things. We know much more about concussions now than we did then. It's so tough; it's not a finite type of injury. It's not something where an orthopedic surgeon can say you're going to be out for x number of days. That's not the way it is with head injuries. It's dealing a lot with the unknown. I think we handle things a lot better now in the way they do it. They're a lot more cognizant of long-term things than they were then. When you suffered a concussion back then, you 'got your bell rung' and you came back. Now we're seeing a lot of our peers that have suffered long-term injuries. It's challenging to watch. We're fortunate; we played in an era when you were becoming more and more aware of the long-term ramifications of things like that.

Getting involved with recovery organizations, that's terrific. When you have a reference point, had an experience, you can speak to it much better. You can tell someone that you can recover from this. But when you've actually recovered from it, it carries a lot more weight. To be able to rely on personal experience, personal reference—doing what we did for as long as we did, you can't accelerate some of the experiences you learned playing the game. You can't coach it, you can't teach it. But you can share it. Some of the veterans that we played with shared a lot of things that were very helpful to me. Brian, having gone through this medically and being able to share it, is invaluable for people.

Learning to adapt and adjust, like changing sides, we were blessed with the lessons we learned in hockey. A lot of the things we learned had nothing to do with sport, they were more about life. When people talk about ability, I think one of the greatest abilities you get in sport is the ability to keep going. That's not a skating talent, or a shooting talent or passing talent—it's merely the ability to keep going. That's something that he's clearly applied to the challenge he's been through with this."

—Dave Poulin, former teammate

"The first thing you think about is my dad [Gordie Howe] had a stroke, so when I did find out about Brian having a stroke, I told him the results that my dad had from doing the stem cell treatments. I strongly believe that Dad would not have lived another two months had he not done that.

Every stroke is different. I've had a couple good friends who have had strokes and the people who are dedicated to it are the ones who have a fighting chance at recovery. The one thing that is most noticeable with Brian is his family background. His father was a reverend and his mother just a wonderful person. To me, that kind of paves the way for the individual. I think in this case, when you need to dig deep, you have to set your mind to what you have to do. Because if you don't do it you're really not going to have a good quality of life.

It's for sure that Brian definitely has many of the qualities that were taught to him by his parents. You have to think positively. There are people who are born with disabilities and there are some like Brian who have health issues during their lifetime. I believe that if you're not in a positive frame of mind, you're not getting out of it. There's just no way. Brian's always had a positive, upbeat way about him. I think the people who know Brian a bit know he was pretty quiet, reserved, and while he was outward with 'Brian Propp–isms,' inwardly you could tell he was a thinker. But he kept a lot of that close to his vest. He was never outspoken, always very respectful of people.

He's always been real positive. I don't think I've ever seen him beat down in all the years we've played together. And if things weren't going well—maybe the media got on him because he wasn't always a physical player, but I never saw it that way. Brian was one of the smartest players, thought the game extremely well, and he had a really good skill set. So why go in a corner with a guy 30 pounds heavier and get the snot beat out of you when you can outthink the guy?

A funny story—when I was still playing with Hartford [in the early '80s], I was playing against Brian in a game at the Spectrum. He speared me in the back of one of my legs. I turned around and whacked him. Then we kind of looked at each other. Then we both started jawing away and neither one of us could fight worth a damn. Next thing you know, his teammates Paul Holmgren, Behn Wilson, and somebody else suddenly appear, and Brian gets behind them and starts chirping away at me. I remember thinking I have to be careful or those three guys are going to kill me! But a year later we were teammates and best buddies.

Brad McCrimmon and Brian had a connection and were great friends. Then Brad and I became partners, so that's how my friendship with Brian got started, right from the first day of training camp in Portland, Maine. Brian was a good teammate and is a good friend of mine.

The thing I respect most about Brian is how he is as a human being, how he treated other people. He's always respectful of other people. When you consider who your friends are, I think of someone I can count on no matter what and Brian is that kind of guy."

—Mark Howe, former teammate

"When I heard the news about [Brian's] health crisis, I was confident he would pull through because he's a stubborn S.O.B. You don't know how really stubborn he is until you've been around him a long time.

I didn't get word until about a week or so. It was almost a month before I saw him. When I first saw him he was still in a wheelchair, pedaling himself around. He's come a long way from that point to where he is now. From what I heard, after the incident, he was practically dead on the floor. Now the only thing that seems to ail him from a physical perspective is his hand. That said, he probably goes out and shoots 80 on the golf course.

I met his dad and mom, and I knew that Brian was always a believer. I knew they were a religious family and Brian used to go to church all the time. He's been a religious guy most of his life. That was his upbringing. I think after the incident he grabbed ahold of anything he could get a hold on. That to me is part of his stubbornness. He was relentlessly stubborn, refused to say no. Ultimately, he had to get back as far as he could get back.

He just wouldn't quit, and that's always the way he's been whenever I've been around him.

If a scout looked at him when he was 16, he probably wasn't the best skater, not the greatest puck-handler, and yet the young man could score 90 goals in a 70-game season. He had true ability. He loved to score goals. He worked real hard at it and was relentless about it. And we had good teams, we were quite lucky to have good teams.

It's nothing short of a mini miracle that he's come back as far as he has. A lot of guys who were in that kind of recovery protocol didn't even make it halfway back.

Today, he's helped educate me and others about strokes. I think it could be just as debilitating as having a heart attack. I think he's a guy who has always given back and that's what he's doing now by helping others in similar situations. The fact that he's now doing it for a cause that he truly believes in is something I think he will always do."

—Ray Allison, childhood friend, former teammate

"One thing I always think is funny is [Brian] can be a very stubborn man. And he was completely stubborn against the stroke. That's probably the best way to describe it. It completely shut his entire body down. He just wasn't having any of it. He fought really hard—from where he was when he first had his stroke, he couldn't move, he couldn't speak. He really couldn't make sounds.

He went from that to being able to be in a place where you wouldn't even know he had a stroke sometimes. It was slow going. He was in the hospital quite a while. I remember visiting him and sometimes he would get a little frustrated that his body couldn't do the things that he wanted it to do. But he never let that get to him. Never gave up. He just basically kept on working harder to make sure he could get back to the best recovery that he could.

I'm basically blown away by how well he actually recovered. He basically blew away every doctor's anticipation for recovery. We even went to see radiologists to review the scans we had received from the hospital. The radiologist that we went to said, 'These scans are from him, right?' Then he added, 'He should have died.' He said there was no way my dad should be alive. 'There's no way he should be anything but a vegetable.'

It's incredible how far he's come back. Most people learning of his story don't actually know how bad it was in the beginning. You see and hear him now, he has mild aphasia, his right hand is a little bit messed up, but I think one thing that people don't know is just how bad it was when it first happened.

Honestly, there was a point where he was going through all these speech therapists where he kind of got to a point where things weren't getting better. It got to the point where it was kind of like, 'Well, I guess the recovery period is over. What you have now is what you're left with.' I just don't think he accepted that. Because there was about a month of stagnant no difference. You could tell at the end of that month he was getting frustrated. He was trying to say things and they weren't coming out.

That's where it probably kicked in right there. He was like, 'OK, apparently everyone is telling me from all the science, like after six months, that's your recovery period. Everything after that is just going to stay.' He proceeded to spend the next three months continuing to get better.

There are stories of people who go through this kind of stuff and then it's something completely different to see it actually happen. Because it's easy to watch a movie and go, 'Oh, there goes the hero, saving the day.' His recovery really sent it home how amazing his physical body is, just the way it was able to rebound, just stay himself. Even through the anger and the ups and downs, he still kept fighting. He just never really gave up, gave in.

The first words he was ever actually able to say were 'Bernie Parent.' That was the only thing he could say. Those were the only words he was able to come up with for two weeks before he started saying other stuff. But even through all of that, he never really changed."

—Jackson Propp, Brian's son

"We were completely different in a lot of ways. The way we first met was I was working at a bar at the Coastline [in Cherry Hill, New Jersey]. When the wives would come in, I would make sure they were taken care of. If you keep the wives happy then the husbands come, and it snowballs into a great thing for the establishment.

I was outgoing—bouncer at a bar, lifeguard at the shore. Here was this quiet kid from a small town in Saskatchewan. We were completely different. But I think he was looking for someone outside the hockey world to befriend somebody. And I just happened to be that guy.

This happened in 1981 or '82.

I think he appreciated humor. He would laugh at stuff hysterically. I have kind of a funny wit to myself. That's where I think we kind of got along. That's also why we got along so well—I wasn't enamored by the whole celebrity thing. I appreciated what they did to get to where they were at, but I just treated them like my other buddies. I think they thought of me as someone who just didn't hang out with them because they were hockey players.

When Ray Allison and I took him out after he had the stroke, it was a tough time for everybody. I said, 'Listen, Ray, let's take him away.' So we went up to the Poconos, went to play golf a couple days and give everyone a break.

He understands his wit is different. I think it has to do with where he grew up. You know, Brian graduated with 13 people in his class. I graduated with 1,050. Completely different worlds. At my five-year reunion, 18 people had already passed away. That's kind of crazy.

It was always inside of him to be more open. Him coming to Philly was probably a great thing in a lot of senses. This was a great place to open the real Brian Propp up.

He's always been upbeat, he's always been a positive person. His support team at the time and also…his outlook has always been positive. He would take something that really didn't mean much to a lot of people and he would make it like, 'Wasn't that great, how that pushed us to this or that!' I think the whole hockey background—you have to push yourself to be better—I think that's what really helped him and also frustrated him. He wants to be better. He felt his training throughout his life—he knew what it took to get to the next level and get back to where he wanted to be.

There were people at Magee [Rehabilitation] who said you might never get back to where you were. People who have had this would let everybody know up front what happened to them but that's not Brian. When I think back to the first day at Magee, he couldn't speak at all. It was really difficult to try to decipher what he was saying. He knew what he wanted to say, there was just a disconnect between his brain and his speech. I could look him in the eye and see that he was expecting us to try to figure out what he was saying.

I was in tears the first time I saw how this affected him. And then as we got going, I started laughing at some of the things he was trying to say. I wasn't laughing at him; I was laughing with him. And he started laughing. He would say, "I know this sounds stupid. But I'm trying." And I said, well just keep trying; we'll figure it out.

Most people would be super frustrated and though he was depressed at times, he just always saw the good in everything. I don't know how much of that was the religion part from the beginning because I didn't know him when he was 12 and how that impacted his life.

I think it's great, the fact that he's looking for ways to try to give back. He's always been that guy that makes up those cards of himself that he gives out. He loves to give them out to people. He's always been a giving guy. I ended up living with him for about a year and a half. Never charged me a dime. Let me help him until he figures out where he's going to go. We became even really closer then. I was the best man in his second wedding, and he was the best man in my wedding.

His giving back is tremendous. To the point where you would think that some people would have to work at that. Not him. Not one bit.

He's a simple guy. He's always trying to help somebody out or do something good for somebody. I think that's what attracted me to him. He's a good-hearted guy and I think we meshed because I think I wasn't necessarily the opposite of him, but I was always thinking let's do something crazy, fun, nutty.

The cruises we went on, there were some crazy stories from those. And let's not forget to mention Howie Mandel and the Guffaw stuff. Here's the real story. I was a lifeguard down the shore and the guys I worked with lived in Linwood. They had a lap pool in their house, which is why they were such great swimmers. We went to their house for a party one night, drinking the whole night. On TV, there was a Howie Mandel special. He was doing the Guffaw. In my drunken state, I just started doing it."

—Scott McKay, close friend

"Brian was extremely determined. Playing in practice, you needed to tell him to stop because he was so determined. All he wanted to do was score, even if it was only practice. He would drive you nuts until he put the puck in the net or until he had enough of it. If he had his mind on something, he was so determined he wasn't going to stop. He was probably one of the best two-way players I ever played with. I would say he was so determined to score to the point where it became a bit unsettling.

Brian wasn't afraid to go to the dirty areas, especially when you consider he wasn't one of the biggest guys out there. When he got his mind on something there, you couldn't change it.

With the recovery, I think he was able to maintain a positive attitude. That's the way he played the game of hockey. With this challenge, he believed he was going to get better. And I think he already had that belief. Once he set his mind to something, he was hard to deter. He knew he was going to do it and he did. That's the kind of guy he always was. That's probably what helped him.

He was a humble guy and a team player. Brian was never a selfish player. Never thought of himself as an individual player."

—Dave Brown, former teammate

"Brian was always a fighter in his own way. When [his stroke] happened at such a relatively young age, we were all kind of shocked. You hear about people at that age having a stroke, but you never think it's going to happen to someone you know. I remember seeing him early after the stroke. When he told me, I think I was with Brad [Marsh], and he tried to tell us, he tried to spit out, 'I'm going to fight, I'm going to beat it.' It was painful to watch but at the same time, you could see the fight and the determination in his eyes, in his facial expression, too. To play as long as he did and achieve what he managed to do, it takes a lot of courage and a lot of fight.

Brian worked hard. You know you don't score that many goals unless you go to those areas where you get cross-checked. Brian had the courage to go to those areas to score. Can you imagine how many goals he would have scored today? The noise from that goal to tie up Game 6 in 1987 against Edmonton felt like it lifted the Spectrum roof a bit. I remember a lot of passes he made to me for empty-net goals in those years. I was very fortunate to be able to play with him."

—Paul Holmgren, Brian's former coach and GM

"Brian was such a consistent player, the numbers that he put up. What I marvel at is he played in all situations, had a two-way game, but he was always consistent at those. He never had three or four bad games in a row. Brian would never go through long slumps. This was a guy who you counted on every day. And he was a big part of those '80s teams.

He was a quiet leader; I loved him because he was a team guy. He had me over to his house a million times for dinner, organizing activities. The way he led was different. He wasn't a hugely vocal guy like a Brad McCrimmon or a Mark Howe, but he did it in a different way. Those teams were very tight, and he was a big part of that tightness.

His recovery doesn't surprise me; it's just part of his work ethic. He's stubborn, but he also loves to live life. He's a people person. As a kid he was shy. But now he lights up a room. I saw at the Flyers Hall of Fame thing, he comes into a room and the whole place gets lit up.

As for helping others, he gives back. Even back in the day, he was always at hospitals, signing stuff for kids. Going to schools—all he does for others doesn't surprise me. He's just that type of guy. Inspiring other people in the same situations. That's Brian Propp. He's just one of those guys that you want to love because he puts his heart and soul in everything he does."

—Rick Tocchet, former teammate

"I think we all felt like Brian could make it through, to be honest with you. The first reaction [after his stroke] was, *Are you kidding?* He was in good shape; he skated several times a week. He was way too young to have something like that happen. So, it was a surprise to begin with. If anybody could deal with what was coming, you knew he could. It is what it is, and he's made the best of it.

Anyone who knows Brian knows he doesn't have a malicious bone in his body. He's a salt-of-the-earth person. It doesn't surprise me. When we became partners on the broadcast, it took him awhile to become comfortable with his role because it didn't fit his personality naturally, but he sure adapted to it. You have to respect what he did as a player. He's one of the greatest players of this franchise's history. So, whenever he and I would disagree about something on the ice, I would defer to him.

As for his work helping others, if you know Brian, it doesn't surprise you at all. He just wants to help people no matter what the situation. He's just that type of person and it doesn't surprise me in the least."

—Tim Saunders, former radio broadcast partner

ANGEL
ON MY WING

A STORY OF FAITH,
DETERMINATION, AND COURAGE

**BRIAN PROPP
WITH WAYNE FISH**

**TRIUMPH
BOOKS**

Copyright © 2024 by Brian Propp and Wayne Fish

No part of this publication may be reproduced, stored in a retrieval system, or transmitted in any form by any means, electronic, mechanical, photocopying, or otherwise, without the prior written permission of the publisher, Triumph Books LLC, 814 North Franklin Street, Chicago, Illinois 60610.

Library of Congress Cataloging-in-Publication Data available upon request.

This book is available in quantity at special discounts for your group or organization. For further information, contact:
   Triumph Books LLC
   814 North Franklin Street
   Chicago, Illinois 60610
   (312) 337-0747
   www.triumphbooks.com

Printed in U.S.A.
ISBN: 978-1-63727-640-2
Photos courtesy of Brian Propp's collection unless otherwise specified

CONTENTS

FOREWORD

WHEN WORD OF A FORMER professional player's life-threatening medical crisis reached the hockey community in 2015, unquestionably there were some who harbored doubts about the individual's chances of recovery to a normal existence.

I wasn't one of them.

My optimism stemmed from having known Brian Propp since he was a raw but promising rookie on the Philadelphia Flyers back in 1979–80.

It took a lot of grit and gumption for a 20-year-old to crack a lineup that went a pro sports record 35 games (25–0–10) without a loss and then battled the budding dynasty New York Islanders to six games before bowing out in the Stanley Cup Final.

Like me, Propp hails from Canada's Midwest, where work ethic and perseverance figure prominently in dinner table talk. Hockey might be a kid's game to some, and a way of making money for others, but in places like Saskatchewan and Manitoba, a lot of it has to do with bettering oneself through determination and purpose.

That's why, when I learned Brian had suffered a massive stroke on September 3, 2015, while vacationing with his family in Annapolis, Maryland, I had a strong belief that if anyone could pull through such an ordeal and make it back on the other side, it was "Propper."

That 1980 team was a tight-knit group, with a number of core players from the two Stanley Cup championship teams of the early 1970s still dotting the roster.

To join that outfit, you had to be pretty damn good.

As a player–assistant coach of that team, I got to know Brian quickly. I learned he hailed from Lanigan, Saskatchewan, and was the son of a minister, the Rev. Reinhold Propp. That alone told me he came from a pretty straightforward household. At an early age, Brian lit up the junior ranks, setting one record after another, particularly in his late teens with the Brandon Wheat Kings.

So, it was no surprise to me when the Flyers used their first-round (14th overall) draft pick to select him. Needless to say, he didn't disappoint. Right out of the gate, you could see not only the skill but the ability to mix it up in the dirty areas. Standing just 5'9" and only weighing in the high 180s, he showed a willingness to bump shoulders both in the corners and in front of the net.

Perhaps those traits played a part in his recovery and rehabilitation after the stroke. I've been told he spent countless hours in therapy, including regular sessions for speech improvement and also hundreds of hours sitting in a hyperbaric/sensory deprivation tank.

After retiring as a player and becoming general manager of the Flyers, I watched Brian blossom into one of the greatest players in team history. He was a key part of those 1985 and 1987 Stanley Cup Final teams that pushed the eventual Stanley Cup championship teams led by Wayne Gretzky and Mark Messier to the limit.

In fact, during that 1987 playoff run, Brian registered a franchise-record 28 points, a mark that stood until Danny Brière posted 30 in the 2009–10 postseason quest.

Later, when I was named general manager of the Minnesota North Stars, I signed Brian because I knew of his veteran leadership. He played a significant role in getting the North Stars all the way to the Cup Final against Mario Lemieux and the Pittsburgh Penguins. While the outcome wasn't what we wanted, Brian enjoyed one of his finest postseasons ever with a total of 23 points in 23 games.

My most vivid memories of Brian's playing days are from those postseason experiences, both on and off the ice.

He scored the tying goal late in the comeback Game 6 against the Oilers in 1987. That marker, along with J.J. Daigneault's game-winner, evoked a roar so loud that many veterans claim it was the most raucous they had ever heard the old Spectrum.

When I learned Brian had collapsed that late summer night in 2015, I thought back to the 1989 Eastern Conference Finals between the Flyers and Montreal Canadiens. In Game 1, defenseman Chris Chelios blindsided Brian with an elbow to the head at the Montreal Forum.

Brian, who had scored 14 goals in his previous 15 games during that postseason, was knocked unconscious, had to be loaded into an ambulance, and was whisked away to a local hospital.

Those who witnessed this incident feared for his life, much less expected him to play hockey again in that series. But after missing only one game, Brian cleared protocol and was ready to go again.

It took courage to jump back into the action of a physical and sometimes violent game—the same kind of fortitude I knew Brian would exhibit in his inspiring recovery from the 2015 health challenge.

If someone up there is indeed watching over Brian, I truly believe he deserves that divine attention.

Bob Clarke is a three-time NHL MVP, two-time Stanley Cup champion, and first-ballot Hockey Hall of Famer who is considered the greatest Flyer in franchise history.

PROLOGUE

EVERYONE HAS DATES in their history that mark life-changing moments, be they for the better or worse.

For some, it can be that first kiss, a straight-A report card, or, on the flip side, missing the final cut of an eventual championship sports team.

I've had many positive experiences in my existence. It would be difficult to pick out just one. But on the negative side, one split second in time stands out beyond all the rest—one that took place early in the fateful morning of September 3, 2015.

Let me explain all the medical challenges and circumstances that led up to that fateful late summer day.

I had been a hockey player from early youth. Hardly anyone who competes in the sport that long gets through without some form of injury or medical condition.

For me, it was Atrial Fibrillation or AFib, a condition known as the most common type of irregular heartbeat, which often causes the heart to beat too quickly. One of the biggest concerns with AFib is the risk of stroke. In fact, people with AFib have approximately five times greater risk of stroke than those who do not have AFib.

I found out I had AFib after my career with the Flyers and other NHL teams. I learned from about the year 2000 on that I had this condition. My physician, Dr. Gary Dorshimer, found it, and what I started to do was take mandatory blood thinners and a small aspirin every day to control the risk of blood clots forming.

It took a little while to control all those levels and get them right. After that, I knew I had to take a blood thinner every day. Doctors told me to be careful not to get another concussion or head injury.

That said, by the time 2005 rolled around, doctors informed me my AFib condition had gotten worse. I underwent some new tests at the University of Pennsylvania, where a team stopped my heart momentarily and then restarted it to get it back on the proper rhythm. I wanted to make sure I was not in AFib again, and it's safe to say a lot of prayers were quietly spoken that morning.

I don't know if that really worked, so it was back to blood thinners and baby aspirin.

That same year I underwent a sleep test in Marlton, New Jersey. It seems I was making more noise in my slumber hours than the 5:05 Amtrak pulling into South Street Station.

Four years later I had something called a heart ablation back at Penn with Dr. Mike Riley. It was a six-hour surgery. They tried to burn the ends of the heart muscle by cauterizing them. It took six months to get the medication set up the correct way.

After about six months, I was able to get off the blood thinners because of the heart ablation. I thought I was good because I wasn't in AFib anymore. After time, though, the medication wore off. That said, I was still in good shape. I still skated a couple days a week in a morning hockey league at Pennsauken Skate Zone in New Jersey.

Around Labor Day 2015, a week before a trip to Annapolis, Maryland, we took the family to visit the U.S. Naval Academy for my son, Jackson. My day-to-day health seemed to take a wrong turn just before this hiatus. I checked into Shore Medical Center, but they didn't find anything. So we decided to go on the trip. In hindsight, that probably wasn't a great idea.

I was feeling OK the first day, but after that I had a really bad headache. We had rented a house, so on the second day, I just stayed in during the afternoon. That night I still had a really bad headache. Something was definitely wrong.

Sometime during the night, my world got turned upside down.

Later I learned I had undergone a massive stroke that affected my heart and my brain in three different places. In the middle of the night I just fell out of bed, hit the side of the bed, and lost a couple teeth. I couldn't talk or walk or do anything.

Thankfully my family was there to call 911 pretty fast.

I stayed in the hospital for five days. From there I was transferred to Magee Rehabilitation in Philadelphia. Safe to say, we got to know each other pretty well. I was there for six weeks, doing three hours per day of occupational and speech therapy, not to mention physical therapy.

Speech therapy took me a long time, because I couldn't talk at all. It took me a year and a half to make any appreciable headway. After time I started getting better. At Magee, I did another daily session of three hours for more than a year and a half. It took me a long time to realize that I couldn't speed things up, as much as I wanted the process to go a little faster.

Being unable to speak made it tough for me to communicate. I learned after time that the brain needs to heal for it to be better for your body. I used to get upset because progress wasn't being made a little faster. But I learned you have to take your time and be patient with your brain.

Whoever came up with the phrase "patience is a virtue" knew what he was talking about. When certain abilities to function properly are suddenly removed, it's not a particularly comfortable place to be. In a sense, even though I had once enjoyed a large support group of family members and friends, I had taken a lot of pride in being able to fend for myself. Now I was in a situation where I had to rely a lot on others, and it required me to make some challenging adjustments.

Some of the things I had taken for granted were gone. At the outset, there were some physical limitations I had to cope with and learn to work around. A task as simple as brushing one's own teeth or tying a shoe needed some tinkering. It became pretty clear right away that all this was going to take time and there weren't going to be any shortcuts.

Even though I was a bit upset with the rate of progress, I kept a positive attitude. I had been that way as an athlete. I wanted to get better. My friends, Flyers alumni, my family, my faith…they made a big difference. I've always been positive, and this was no different. I had faith that I could get back to normal.

So after my stroke I just kind of took my time. After a year, I was ready for something called the "Watchman" surgery on my heart. Dr. David Collins headed up the surgical team at the University of Pennsylvania. They implanted a device to control my AFib.

I can't say enough about the medical personnel throughout Philadelphia, especially at the University of Pennsylvania. They've been professional every step of the way. The key thing here is no two patients are exactly alike, so treatment is personalized to meet the unique individual's needs.

Ever since that day, September 3, 2015, I've wondered why I pretty much circumnavigated a situation that could have been a lot worse.

Maybe it has something to do with the power of positive thinking. Perhaps it's because I believe that all this isn't just random existence but rather something to do with purpose.

When people ask if it ever occurred to me that my life as I know it might be over at age 56, I smile, shrug my shoulders, and say, "I knew it wasn't my time because I haven't met my grandchildren yet."

CHAPTER 1

A DAD FOR ALL SEASONS

A LOT OF CHILDREN grow up thinking their father can show them the path to the best, most righteous way of life. Those elders tend to lead by example. Live the right way and the next generation will pick up on that with few words needing to be spoken.

So it was with my family growing up in the 1960s in the Canadian province of Saskatchewan. We were just your regular Midwest plains unit, with a mom, a dad, and five children.

Only there was a bonus. My father, Reinhold, was an ordained Lutheran minister. Some of his teachings were rooted in his German heritage, but his way of teaching life lessons was by no means heavy-handed. If you abided by certain social standards, the rest came rather easily.

Oh, and there was a second jackpot as well. My dad was a natural-born hockey enthusiast. Played it, watched it, talked it— ate, drank, and dreamt about it.

He taught me how to play hockey. He was a really good player when he was younger. He could have been drafted by one of the NHL teams but decided to go into the ministry. On open outdoor ice, with the wind swirling in all directions, he was as fast as they come.

My dad started playing in Jansen, Saskatchewan. After I was born in 1959, we moved to Neudorf in the early 1960s. There were five little Propps running—and skating—around in those days. We all looked up to our dad, a towering figure even to adults. He was a 6'2", 200-pound enforcer with a wicked hip check. But he was also sound in the other fundamentals of the game, such as passing the puck.

In all honesty, nearly everything I learned about hockey came from him, whether it was shooting the puck, passing it, or knowing where to be on the ice in both offensive and defensive situations. He taught me to do everything right. One of the things he stressed to me, as a forward, was the importance of playing defense, as well as how to shoot the puck with a purpose and try to hit the net every time.

There were only about 300 people in the town, so it was difficult to gather enough players to form a competitive team. To put it mildly, it was kind of tough to put a team together. We played outside on the ponds but when it got to 40 below zero, we headed indoors.

My dad was really good about supporting me. He didn't pressure me. He did everything well. I learned from him because he was a great coach. Some of the lessons I was taught included how to be humble, how to give back, and how to do everything the right way.

I sang in the church choir for a couple years. When I started playing some pretty serious hockey at around age 15, I couldn't drive, so my parents had to drive me to practices and games. Some of those trips were 20 miles away. And then there were times when we took a bus and there was a bit of guesswork on the departure times. There were no cell phones in the '70s, so we were somewhat on our own.

I grew up with faith. I tend to be more positive. I don't have to tell people now about my health. I know I'm believing. It makes a difference because when I go to church now, I see people that I meet who know what it's all about and how faith helps me to be healthy.

My father preached in English and German every Sunday. That made going to church each Sunday rather special. He was a great guy. He talked to everybody. He visited hospitals. He would spend extra time with people who had challenging illnesses.

My dad taught me to be a Christian. He showed me how to be a good person. I can't stress how important that approach has been over the last nine transformational years of my life.

My father's Sunday message was something people both liked and appreciated. He always put people first, so he knew how to get his beliefs through to them. In turn, he was held in high regard by those who took those emotions to heart.

Saturday nights were spent making final preparations for his moments on Sunday morning before the people. He was good at reaching out to families and talking about things like baseball and hockey. When you have five kids, you become somewhat of an expert on those subjects. There was a lot going on. He could talk about the people who were involved in those sports and how it made a difference in the community.

My brother Greg and I would help out with the church bulletins on Saturday night as well. The printing machine was hand powered. It had an old-fashioned crank. The ink was held in the center of the cylinder. After that, you had to let the ink dry, then fold the bulletins in quarters. We had about 50. This gave us a chance to help out and feel like we were doing something to contribute to our father's life's work.

It was nice to be in church every Sunday renewing my faith in the Lord. My father always taught us to be humble and do the right things. Those lessons have stayed with me to this day, and a lot of that is because my dad was my role model.

On Sunday morning, after the donation plate was passed around and all the money was collected, we had to count everything. I was sort of like a young accountant, writing everything down.

I just loved collecting old coins. They might have just been nickels, dimes, and quarters, but I was able to take out some that were worthwhile and replace them with my own money. There was something about collecting old coins that really appealed to me. To this day, I still enjoy finding weathered coins and occasionally checking to see how much value they still have.

While all this was going on, my mom was busy teaching Sunday school. She had all the kids until they reached confirmation at age 13 or 14. She also taught piano, so of course I had to learn how to play that instrument. Sometimes I had to play in front of other people. One time I just didn't want to do it, and I really got in bad trouble because of that. I knew how to play but for some reason I just didn't have it that day. My dad didn't get mad that often, but boy, he sure wasn't happy that day. The belt came off and a little corporal punishment was in order. So the piano playing definitely picked up after that.

Part of my mom's duties included overseeing the church choir. I wasn't a very good singer, so I sort of faked it by just mouthing the words but not making too much sound. We had a conversation about it, but after time she just gave up. I don't blame her. My heart just wasn't in it.

It didn't help that my sister Angela was a great organ player. All five of us had to play the piano, and she just took it to another level.

There was a building next to the church and upstairs was a large seating area with a stage. Downstairs, there was a kitchen.

I loved it because they also had a ping-pong table. So I was able to practice ping-pong a lot after school, and I got really good. By the time I reached 10th grade, I won the high school tournament. Only about 90 kids competed, but still—quite an accomplishment, or so I thought at the time.

As far as my faith goes, with each passing year I felt stronger about my belief in the Lord. I still have a bible that I read every once in a while. My dad gave it to me when I was young. I like to read from that occasionally just to concentrate a little bit more with faith. I try to read a little bit each day to concentrate on life and the challenges it presents. That reading really helped me to get better.

I know after my stroke, it made a difference for me just because having my family being there, along with the faith, made a difference with my thoughts and how I could get better.

———————

The five young Propps were all born in a short time frame. My older brother, Greg, was born in 1957. After I hit town in 1959, my sister Angela arrived in 1960. She was followed by Carol in 1961 and then Ron in 1962.

If there was any question about my heritage, all you had to do was meet my grandmother. She only spoke German. She lived with us when we were little kids. She made it all the way to age 94 before calling it a life.

Neudorf was your typical Midwest farming village. One main street, which wasn't paved, with one store plus a Chinese restaurant and a pool hall where everyone shot pocket billiards. Most people got haircuts once a week. Just about what one would expect from a little town in what some would say was the middle of nowhere.

Skating was a big part of local activity. You did that in the winter, went to school in the summer. It was a pretty simple life.

As I mentioned, my dad was really good with people. He would visit people in hospitals, mainly at Melville, necessitating a 20-mile drive. This would happen during the week. He would drive over and say hi. He would have coffee with them. He just loved his coffee. Although he didn't partake of too much alcohol, he did have a decided cigarette habit. When the five of us kids got a little older, he pretty much stopped cold turkey when he discovered some of us were "borrowing" some of his smokes.

Coaching was a big part of his hockey repertoire. He could spot strengths and weaknesses in everyone's game. When he played senior hockey, he was kind of a tough guy and apparently earned instant respect among his peers. His physical game came naturally. Eventually he had to give up the game because some parishioners thought he played a little too rough. I don't think he was trying to hurt anyone, but it just seemed to be a bit of a contradiction—this man of the cloth preaching kindness on Sundays but not a lot of kindness during games on other days of the week.

Meanwhile, my mom, Margaret, had her five kids at a fairly early age, so once we were grown there was time for a career as a court reporter. Greg was a master mechanic, starting at the ripe old age of 17. He initially worked for Hauser Chevrolet-Oldsmobile, then joined SaskPower as a heavy-duty mechanic. From there it was on to a position with TransGas as an industrial mechanic, then a transition to SaskEnergy (natural gas) as a supervisor. All three entities were under the same crown corporation. Later he joined Hundseth Power Line Construction, which deals with tele-communication and power line construction.

Both Greg and I left home when we were 17. I was on my way to play for the WHL Brandon Wheat Kings. Angela was always good with business, and now she's an organic farmer. In addition, the family operates a white-tailed deer hunting camp near the Carrot River. Carol continues her career as a schoolteacher. I'm told she's an excellent teacher with the younger age groups. Ron, well-versed in IT, has followed me to the Philadelphia area.

Whether we've wound up far from home or still live in or around Neudorf, the memories of our upbringing are still vivid. I recall going to school where there were as few as five kids in a class. Mine graduated with about 10. It goes without saying everybody knew everybody but it made for some great friendships.

My first job was delivering newspapers when I was 13. The story behind that is I would walk across yards throughout town delivering the papers. There was this one house where the guy owned a big German shepherd, which he kept on a big chain. I figured everything was safe but then one day, when I hopped the fence and was delivering a paper, the dog managed to break the chain and attacked me pretty good. He got ahold of my arm and chomped down. I had to get several stitches, and it goes without saying I was more than a little scared. I was not real friendly with dogs after that.

Kids in Neudorf did more than eat lunch at noon hour. They would jump into their skates and play until the afternoon school bell rang at 1 o'clock. It was just a simple life. No one knew what was going on half the time. It was very relaxing. When it got to 30 below zero, we didn't know any better. You just had to dress for it.

After school, we would head for the pool hall to shoot a game or three. A rack only cost 10 cents. If I do say so myself, I became a pretty good pool player. Maybe not a shark, because I wasn't trying to hustle people. But good enough to earn respect among the town's best shooters. There was so much free time you could really work on your game. It was just something to do to pass the time. Other than that, the summer afternoons were spent baling hay, working on the farms and making a little extra money. It was tough work, and it lasted all day. The pay wasn't great—around a dollar an hour. But who cared? Most of us were content with that. It built character because you wanted to work and make some money.

My best friend in Neudorf was a kid named Dave Edgar. He lived on a farm about 15 miles outside of town. When I was about 15 years old, I jumped on his bike and went down a steep hill, lost control, and hit my head. After a quick trip to the doctor's office, I walked out with stitches in my skull and a red face to boot. That wasn't one of my better days. Dave and I were best friends and would play ping-pong every day at noon. We were competitors at school, and we won the Saskatchewan fast pitch title when we were 16. It was a kick to win the local tournament.

———————

Anyone who stopped by the Propp household for dinner got more than just a meal. They witnessed what might be best described as a ritual, which had its serious and not-so-serious moments. Remember, this family had an ordained minister at the head of the table and five children with a lot of pent-up energy. There were bound to be some special moments.

One day, my sister Carol, who was about seven or eight at the time, reminded everyone of her love for ketchup in a rather graphic way. We were having dinner and she reached for the ketchup bottle and decided she was going to squeeze it to release her favorite condiment. Well, at first, the bottle wasn't cooperating. After several failed attempts at normal pressure, she really gave it a two-hander. Unfortunately, the bottle was aimed right at our father. Of course, a big squirt of ketchup went airborne and landed right on our dad, who was dressed pretty well, as usual.

He was really upset about that, at least for a moment. Then he realized it was an accident and not an intentional act. You should have heard the laughter. Initially, that made him a little angrier. But eventually he came around and it became a fun memory.

After dinner we would take turns washing the dishes, usually alternating between the girls and the boys. No dishwasher in those days, my friend. Hey, even that could be entertaining because we were just simple farm children.

These might be modern times, but at the Propp dinner table today, no cell phones are allowed. The idea is to conduct oneself in a respectful manner and join in the conversation when called upon. I would venture to say it was really good for your mental well-being. No need to know what the heck is happening on TikTok. When I was back in Saskatchewan at the end of summer 2023, my sister and her family used the same guidelines. They all eat together. No phones. There's prayer before the start of every meal. It's so nice to have this sort of discipline because it goes against today's norm of everyone staring at the little black rectangle.

At our house in Neudorf, we raised a lot of our own food. We had an oversized garden with peas, carrots, corn—you name it, we had it. Then we also had potatoes. We had a unique way of getting rid of the dreaded potato bugs. Just pick them off the plants with your fingers and drive over them with our truck. We squished them pretty good and enjoyed that.

We lived in a parsonage, and it was right next to the church. The next building was a hall where my mom, who was a Sunday school teacher, provided us with a little more religion.

Playing ball was the big summertime activity. With five kids in the family, we pretty much had our own team. It should be noted we often played ball outside the building adjacent to the church. Lots of windows and plenty of batted balls…what could possibly go wrong? I don't know how many times the window on the garage shattered because of errant throws and batted balls. That was another thing we got to have some fun with.

When the temperatures turned cold in the wintertime in Neudorf we played street hockey. It was an everyday thing. I can remember when Dave Wendel, a good hockey player, would join us and we would play for hours until my mom would call us for dinner.

Even though I had what one might call a religious upbringing, that still didn't stop me from challenging the system…in a bad way.

One time I stole a Kit Kat candy bar. It couldn't have sold for more than a dime, but thievery is thievery. I got caught and man, was I in deep trouble with the manager. First I had to confess to my dad what I had done. Needless to say, that didn't go over very well. Quite a contradiction when the man who spread God's word on Sunday was being forced to speak to his son about stealing stuff on Tuesday. I had to pay it back and apologize to the manager, which was rather humiliating. Did I ever learn a lesson from that particular incident. There would be no more stealing in my future.

My dad was also the hockey coach, and my goal-scoring prowess kind of put both of us in an awkward spot. In one game when I was eight years old, I scored 15 goals in the first two periods. Fifteen! We didn't have much competition. I didn't know when to stop. So my dad called me over and told me, "No more shooting at the net. For the last period, just pass the puck to one of your teammates." I could have scored a lot more goals but we kind of just knew better than that. It was the Christian thing to do.

Later, when I was with the Melville Millionaires, I always wore a purple turtleneck sweater underneath my regular jersey. It kept me warm. I got known for that. It probably added to the "local legend" thing. We already had signs around the town announcing which celebrities hailed from the area. One before my time was Eddie Litzenberger, who played for Chicago, Montreal, Detroit, and Toronto. Jarret Stoll, who played for the Oilers, Kings, Rangers, and Wild, once competed in Neudorf. My mom's curling team was also the best in the province.

CHAPTER 2

KING OF THE WHEAT KINGS

JUNIOR HOCKEY ISN'T just a stepping stone to the professional game. It's a place where you mature, form friendships, and learn a lot of life lessons.

And so it was with me and the Western Hockey League's Brandon Wheat Kings. The WHL might not have the glamorous history of the Ontario Hockey League or the Quebec Major Junior Hockey League, but it certainly had its fair share of bona fide superstars.

After the success I enjoyed with the Melville Millionaires, there was nothing to suggest I wouldn't continue that career path in the WHL. And the next three years did nothing to dispel that notion. We played unbelievable hockey, capped off by winning the WHL title in 1979.

Dunc McCallum, our coach, was a 15-year veteran of the professional hockey wars. He played in 187 NHL games for the New York Rangers and Pittsburgh Penguins and later another 100 split between the AHL Chicago Cougars and Houston Aeros. While he had enjoyed success with those teams, it wasn't until he came home to his native Manitoba to coach the Wheat Kings that he really stood out.

Over five seasons, he compiled a record of 251–123–41, good for a .654 winning percentage. That's the highest success number in the history of the league. He was a two-time coach of the year recipient and did more than just shout orders on the bench or in the locker room. No, he was genuinely interested in the career path of each of his young players. He instilled both knowledge and the ability to gain confidence by executing a system to the letter.

He taught us how to do well, outwork other teams. I was lucky. I arrived the same time he did, and there seemed to be mutual respect right from the get-go. At the same time, I was surrounded by a lot of future NHL stalwarts, including the late Brad McCrimmon, Ray Allison, Bill Derlago, Laurie Boschman, Dave Semenko, Glen Hanlon, and Walt Poddubny. You name it, we had at least a good—if not great—player at every position.

In my first season in Brandon the Wheat Kings only lost 12 games. Our line of Derlago, Allison, and myself finished No. 1 in league scoring. Everything seemed to go right, even in the playoffs, where I posted 14 goals and 26 points in just 16 games. A lot of that had to do with the guys I was playing with on a nightly basis. You could see even then that players like my two linemates were going to enjoy future success in the NHL.

It only got better from there. In the 1977–78 campaign, the Wheat Kings lost only eight games. Not only did I win the regular season scoring title with 70 goals and 112 assists for 182 points, but I also registered a whopping 200 penalty minutes to finish among the league leaders in that dubious category. Maybe this was an omen I would be joining the Broad Street Bullies of Philadelphia Flyers infamy in a couple years.

When the season ended, I was voted league MVP.

Then, the following year, we lost only five games the entire season. That's a record that still stands today and a source of great pride among team alumni. Our revamped line of Boschman, Allison, and myself was the league's top-scoring unit. I finished with 94 goals and 100 assists for 194 points. It was pretty much a given I would win the WHL's MVP a second straight season.

But it wasn't a completely happy ending. We went to the Memorial Cup (Canada's junior championship) and made it all the way to the finals. The title game was one for the ages, back and forth, up and down the ice. Fittingly, the title game went to overtime. Someone had to win, and it wasn't us. From an individual standpoint, I couldn't complain. For the postseason I had 15 goals and a total of 38 points in 22 games.

It's safe to say Dunc played a big role in our success. He was strong on sound positional play, something that came in handy for me in my next stop—the NHL. Dunc skated us hard, made us really work at it. During the season we hardly lost. It was a team on which you wanted to come in every day and give it your best effort.

Having Brad McCrimmon on the team certainly made a big difference. He and Ray Allison really taught me how to be a leader. When I first walked in the door back in 1976, I was real quiet and didn't say much. I just did what I had to in order to put the puck in the net.

With the Wheat Kings based in Manitoba, the geography wasn't favorable for us. A couple times a season we would play games in Winnipeg, which was closer, but other than that, the closest location was Regina and even that was a six-hour drive from Brandon. We were on the bus a lot of the time. That might not sound appealing to many people, but we were young and made the best of the situation.

Trying to make the best of a challenging situation, we would put two seats together, load a mattress on them, and add a sleeping bag on top. Guys would sleep in shifts. There's a bit of a trust factor there and that's how we became really close because we spent a lot of time on that damn bus.

My brother Ron joined the WHL Regina Pats in 1978–79. The story there is we were playing a game against the Pats one night and one of my teammates, Dave Chartier, took a questionable run at Ron. Well, the first rule of thumb in the Propp household is "family first." So I approached Chartier and expressed my displeasure with his actions. I told him, "I don't care what you do out there; just don't hit my brother dirty!" I admit I gave him some grief because I was upset with the way he was acting. I wanted to protect my brother.

Otherwise, the whole three-year experience was pretty much a lot of fun. My first year, in one game I scored seven goals. That was a good way to get started.

The redeeming value of scoring a hat trick or more in a game is the confidence it provides when maybe just getting one or two goals in a really close game can make the difference. Even when the score gets out of hand, just keep trying different moves and make a mental note of what works and what doesn't.

That's why you see guys practice things like breakaways or shootout moves on non-game days. The whole idea is to craft a go-to shot that you can count on when it comes down to crunch time. Scoring seven goals is fun, but if you can take one or two shifty efforts away from that performance, that's what makes it a productive experience.

At the same time, when you become a legitimate threat to score goals, it opens up things for your linemates. I can't tell you how many times as a kid I would pull two defenders toward me and that would free up one or two other guys on my line. Setting up a teammate for a fancy goal is about as gratifying as it gets. You can tell by watching all the smiles when teammates gather together right after scoring a big goal.

At this point I should mention how important Brad McCrimmon was for me in those early years. For one thing, he always had a car. The hockey players billed with other families, and my first year the only mode of transportation I had was my own two feet. The initial year I lived with a schoolteacher and the last two with a farm family. I walked all the time to the rink, about a mile or so.

There were days when it was really cold, so any time I could catch a ride with Brad it made a difference because I didn't have to walk all the time. Also, I was trying to find time to study and eventually I was proud to announce I had graduated from Neelin High School in Brandon.

While Brandon, a town of about 35,000, did have some night-life, we couldn't drink in the bars. So instead we got our hands on some beer and put together some house parties, which were probably more fun anyway.

With the Wheat Kings having exceptional seasons between 1977 and '79, there was a lot of buzz about the fledgling World Hockey Association, a professional rival of the NHL. The WHA was nearing the end of its run but still trying to recruit some headline talent from the junior ranks.

A lot of us were talking about playing in the WHA prior to the 1978–79 season. The WHA still had some credibility. It had the legendary Gordie Howe and some of his sons, including future Hall of Famer Mark, who became a good friend of mine in later years, as well as headliners like Bobby Hull.

Brad, Ray, and I gave some serious thought to playing in the WHA. We would have been paid at least $60,000 if we had jumped to the maverick league. But we decided to stay put and play one more season with Brandon. I was kind of immature, and I don't know if I would have been ready for the pro game at that point. I could have made some more money but, as it turned out, that extra year gave us more time to be some of the top players in the history of Canada junior hockey.

Staying that extra year might have clinched my recognition as the top left wing in Canadian junior hockey history. They announced a list in 1999. On it were Denis Potvin, Guy Lafleur, Mario Lemieux, Bobby Orr, Brian Kilrea, and Bernie Parent, among others. Quite an honor.

CHAPTER 3

A STREAK FOR THE AGES

W HEN I SHOWED UP for my first training camp at the University of Pennsylvania's Class of 1923 Ice Rink in fall 1979, I knew the Flyers were still a pretty good hockey team. After all, they were only four years removed from their second straight Stanley Cup in 1975.

But I wouldn't be telling the truth if I said anyone had any idea this club would go 12 weeks without a loss. It just didn't seem possible anyone could break the Montreal Canadiens' incredible 28-game unbeaten streak set in the 1977–78 campaign.

Don't get me wrong; there was still a lot of talent left over from the glory years, including captain Bobby Clarke and his sniper linemates Reggie Leach and Bill Barber. Those guys alone made the Philly outfit a dangerous one.

After the Flyers selected me 14th overall in the '79 NHL Entry Draft, I guess expectations surrounding me were pretty high. Coach Pat Quinn must have seen something in me that maybe some others didn't, else why would I wind up on a line with Clarke and Leach, essentially breaking up the vaunted LCB (Leach, Clarke, Barber) unit?

In my first game of the 1979–80 season we played the New York Islanders. I managed to score the game-winning goal and added an assist. It was one heck of a way to start, especially against Hall of Fame goaltender Billy Smith. I was feeling pretty good about it and so were my teammates. Maybe a little too good. The second game we went down to Atlanta and promptly got burned by the Flames to the tune of 9–2.

I was thinking, *Wow, is this the way it's going to be in the NHL?* Up one night and down the next? Well, that feeling only lasted a day or two because the next game we started a 35-game (25–0–10) unbeaten streak, which remains a professional sports record to this day. With the five-minute overtime/shootout rule now in place, it will take a team 36 consecutive victories to erase our record from the books. Our record probably won't be broken because there's a lot of balance in the league and with the salary cap, the years of dynasties like the Islanders and Oilers are a thing of the past.

The 1979–80 Flyers team was the perfect blend of youth, experience, toughness, and smarts. Quinn chose to put Barber on a second line with Kenny Linseman at center and Paul Holmgren at right wing. Veteran Rick MacLeish was placed on another line with Al Hill and Tom Gorence. That fourth line of Mel Bridgman, Bob Kelly, and John Paddock (along with Dennis Ververgaert) was a burr under any team's saddle. On defense, it was a good blend of savviness and toughness. Jimmy Watson was paired with Behn Wilson, then came switchable pairings of Mike Busniuk, Frank Bathe, Bob Dailey, Norm Barnes, and André "Moose" Dupont. In goal, it was rookie Pete Peeters and veteran Phil Myre.

Everyone on all four lines seemed to contribute, whether it was on offense or defense. It was amazing because everyone not only knew their role and accepted it but even embraced it.

As potent as those Stanley Cup teams were, this version of the Flyers knew how to score fast and often. We were still learning how to put the puck in the net and at the same time not get scored upon. The perfect example was the fourth game of the season against Montreal. We put up six goals against the Habs and were leading 6–4 late in the game. But we must have fallen asleep because we let the Rouge, Blanc, et Bleu score twice late for a 6–6 tie.

We always had trouble with the St. Louis Blues, and during the streak that didn't change. In Game 14, we had to pull up our socks and somehow hung on for a 3–3 tie. At this point, going after a record was not the first thought on our minds.

Another game that really tested us was Game 17 against Edmonton. This was the Oilers' first season in the NHL, but with Wayne Gretzky and Mark Messier in place, nothing could be taken for granted. We were a little lucky to come away with a 2–2 tie. Looking back, this was one of the games where we were fortunate not to come away with a loss.

Then things started to lighten up a bit on the ice. Off the ice, people were starting to pay attention. Whenever a team or an individual approaches a record, there is all sorts of speculation about whether the mark will be broken and, if so, where that team belongs in the history books.

Road games were especially electric because each team wanted to end the streak on their home ice. The media started following us much closer and that made it that much tougher from Game 20 and on.

That Game 20 was played in Toronto, the hockey media capital of the world. With the game being played in Canada, everybody but the family dog knew we were on an eye-opening streak. Everybody wanted to end it—not just the Maple Leafs players but the fans, too. It really made a difference because it was getting all the press and every team wanted to be the one to end it. That game wound up in a 4–4 tie.

The next game, against Detroit, also ended in a 4–4 tie. There was no rest for the targeted Flyers. Next up was a rambunctious

Bruins team. That game finished in a 2–2 tie, and we were lucky to get back to the dressing room in one piece.

Over those last dozen or so games there were some real nail-biters. Game 24 was played against Chicago and ended in a 4–4 tie. That was the last opponent we wanted to end our streak.

Now we could see the Canadiens' record in sight. In mid-December, playing against the Rangers, fans were on pins and needles. The game ended in a 1–1 tie. This was one of the tougher games. Neither side wanted to give an inch. If they had played overtime in those days, that would have been a good one.

For the record-tying Game 28, we had to play at Pittsburgh, and we couldn't buy a goal. We were down 1–0 until the last five minutes when, lo and behold, MacLeish scored. The man who had shot the puck and led to MacLeish's game-winning deflection in the series-clinching Game 6 of the 1974 Stanley Cup against Boston was at it again. There was laughter in the Flyers locker room after that one.

Then it was on to Boston for a Saturday afternoon game at "the Gahden" to establish the new record in Game 29. The old Boston Garden was already a tough place for Philadelphia to play on its own, let alone with the prospect of a new record. Somehow we did it, winning by a comfortable 5–2 margin.

On the jubilant plane ride home, coach Quinn was a bit out of character with his off-the-cuff comments. I remember him saying how impressive the streak was and that no one in the Flyers organization anticipated this sort of notoriety. He gave the highest praise you can give a team when he said not a single opponent in the streak had outworked the Flyers yet.

I still remember Clarke scoring just six minutes into the game and that took the Garden crowd right out of it. Then our fore-checking took over. Even though the Flyers came into the game having won just four of their previous 30 contests at Boston

Garden, you could feel the confidence level on the Orange and Black bench. We were ahead by only a goal in the third period, but Jimmy Watson scored a rare goal and that took the pressure off.

The whole thing in Boston was pretty amazing. We knew they really wanted to beat us and keep us from breaking the record, but we just played too well.

After that game we just were able to cruise a bit. Game 31 ended in a 4–4 tie with Hartford, which didn't have anything to lose. At this point we knew we were in a rough patch. On the upcoming schedule, we saw we were headed to Minnesota to play the North Stars in early January, and we had a hunch the streak was about to end.

That Boston game had started a stretch of seven games out of eight on the road, and we knew the streak had to end sometime. It's hard enough to win—or in the case of the 1979–80 Flyers, tie—16 straight games on the road.

On January 4, 1980, we headed into Madison Square Garden and beat the New York Rangers 5–3 to extend the streak to 34 games and surpass the Los Angeles Lakers' all-time professional unbeaten streak of 33 games. The difference was there were no ties in NBA basketball, so all 33 of Los Angeles' successes were victories.

After winning 4–2 on January 6, 1980, at Buffalo to extend the streak to 35 games, we kind of ran out of gas and looked like it a couple nights later when we headed to Minnesota. The North Stars were waiting for us in the Twin Cities, and we were quickly dispatched by a 7–1 score. In some ways, we were glad it was over and we didn't have to worry about keeping the streak alive. And at least it didn't end on some crazy bounce goal in the last few seconds of regulation time.

Some impressive numbers came out of the streak. We set team records for longest home undefeated streak at 26 games

(October 11 to February 3) and longest road undefeated streak at 16 games (October 20 to January 6).

We loved what we were doing. I was a rookie, but I couldn't help but think about the years ahead, like, *This is going to be a lot of fun.* In the 35 games, I registered at least 25 points, just one behind captain Clarke. Linseman and Bridgman also had high point totals. Everyone contributed. It was a great time, one of the best of my career.

After the loss, we said to ourselves, "We never want to lose two games in a row for the rest of the season." And guess what? For the remainder of the campaign, we lost back-to-back games only once: March 23 and 25, to Boston and the Islanders.

I'll never forget a lot of what happened my rookie season. No doubt, the team's success paved the way for my career in the NHL. It gave me great confidence that I could get the job done.

That team is one for the books. We had seven players in the NHL All-Star Game in Detroit's Joe Louis Arena. Detroit legend Gordie Howe was in that game. I played against him, and I will always remember the ovation he got. It lasted for minutes. Later, I was put with my Flyers teammate Reggie Leach along with Phil Esposito. I had a goal and an assist.

Later we went to the Stanley Cup Final. What a way to start a career.

CHAPTER 4

THE BIG IRISHMAN

TALK ABOUT LUCKY. When I arrived at Philadelphia Flyers training camp for the first time as a rookie in late summer 1979, I was blessed to have a tough but fair coach waiting to start what would be his first full season with the team. It didn't take me long to figure out that while Pat Quinn could growl with the best of them, he really cared about his players, young or old.

Of course, having succeeded former coach Bob McCammon late in the 1978–79 campaign with mixed results, few would have guessed that this coach and this team would basically start the season on a still-professional-sports-record unbeaten streak of 35 games (25–0–10) and go all the way to the Stanley Cup Final against the New York Islanders.

I didn't know much about Quinn when I hit the city. I was aware they called him "the Big Irishman" and that once he was off the bench it was hard not to find him not smoking one of his favorite cigars. Someone told me he was a 6'3", 215-pound, hard-hitting defenseman for Toronto, Vancouver, and Atlanta. During the 1969 Stanley Cup playoffs, when he was a rookie, he started a bench-clearing brawl when he executed a textbook body check on All-World defenseman Bobby Orr, knocking him unconscious and provoking both the Maple Leafs' and Boston Bruins' benches to jump onto the ice to have at it.

Quinn learned a lot of his coaching acumen from the legendary Fred Shero, serving as his assistant on the Flyers' bench during the 1977–78 season. Shero had piloted the Flyers' two Stanley Cup championship teams in 1974 and 1975 and was known for being a deep thinker and somewhat of an innovator. While he had beaten the Russians in the famous 1976 game at the Spectrum, he did study their methods and strategies, and no doubt Pat was interested in that sort of deep study.

I was immediately struck by Quinn's intelligence pertaining to the game of hockey. He was an excellent teacher and, besides that, he had Bobby Clarke, who had been captain of the team, as an assistant coach. There's nothing like having your best player also be your right-hand man. The two got along quite well and everyone knew they were on the same page.

An example of this came with the way the coaching staff handled speedy center Ken Linseman. Linseman was a bit of a free spirit and tended to do things on his own schedule. There were times—a lot of them—when he didn't pay attention at meetings. Quinn and Clarke had to keep after him. If you have to keep repeating yourself over and over and over again, it gets tiring after a while. And I played quite a few games on a line with "the Rat" and had firsthand knowledge of what was going on.

I started that season on a line with Clarke. But that experiment was short-lived. It was Pat's decision to reunite the famous "LCB" line of Clarke, Bill Barber, and Reggie Leach, which had been so pivotal in the 1975 Stanley Cup Final series win over Buffalo. Quinn decided to assemble a new line with me, Linseman, and tough guy Paul Holmgren. They even gave it a nickname, the "Rat Patrol" line, probably named after the popular TV series of the same name and because "the Rat" was Kenny's nickname.

Quinn's invention worked. I set a Flyers franchise rookie record for goals (34) and points (75). Holmgren had his best year in the NHL with 30 goals and became the first American-born player to score a hat trick in a Stanley Cup Final series. But perhaps most surprising of all, Linseman led the team in both regular season and playoff scoring. Who knew?

The myth behind the Rat nickname was that everyone thought of Linseman as a dirty player, a cheap-shot artist. But Linseman actually picked up the moniker because of his hunched, bent-over skating style. What a year he had, and Quinn deserves a lot of credit for that. He gave Linseman some leeway, and Linseman responded with 79 points along with 107 penalty minutes, plus 22 points in only (because of injuries) 17 playoff games.

Kenny would constantly mess up drills in practice, but Paul and I weren't much better. So Pat would make us do them over and over again. It was a test of wills. We knew we could do better and so did Pat, which is why he invested so much time in us. It was basic stuff—breakouts, power plays, penalty kills. We kind of knew what was going on. Through it all, Pat was quiet. That is, unless you crossed him. Then you knew you were in trouble.

At the same time, it was hard to find fault with the team's results that season. A two-and-a-half-month stretch without a loss can buy you a lot of credibility, regardless of how you practiced. We lost a game early in the season in October, then didn't lose again until January.

Quinn spent a lot of time preparing us for upcoming opponents. He would point out strengths and weaknesses. Perhaps this sort of analysis laid the groundwork for one of his outside interests, the law. A few years later, after he was let go by the Flyers, he remained in the Philadelphia area to attend law school at Widener University and later earned his degree.

I loved Pat. He had all the qualities you would want in a coach. When he walked into a room, his physical presence and powerful features would intimidate the most feared players. Early on, he pulled me aside and gave me some words of encouragement. He knew I liked to go out and have a good time. Then he told others, "I don't care what Brian Propp does; he scores a lot, so I don't mind if he drinks a lot of beer. As long as he performs." I wasn't that bad of a drinker, although I did spend my share of hours at places like Kaminski's (in south Jersey).

It was nice to get drafted when I did (14th overall in 1979) because it gave me a chance to play for Quinn and start my career with the Flyers. Having the right people around you makes a difference. If I had been drafted earlier, say top 10, it probably would have been by a team that ultimately wasn't going to make the playoffs for a couple years.

The key for players like me was to earn the respect of a coach such as Quinn. If you don't have a long résumé of accomplishments at the NHL level, the process takes a while. You develop trust by playing the game the right way and following the game plan.

Maybe the reason that streak happened was because Quinn had Clarke leading the way on the ice. If a player wasn't adhering to the system, there was a good chance he was going to hear about it before he reached the bench.

In later years, I kept in touch with Pat. After my playing career, when I was doing games on the radio, I would say hi to him all the time because I knew he still lived in Pennsylvania. I was glad to learn he had been posthumously inducted into the Hockey Hall of Fame in 2016.

That 1979–80 season was one of the highlights of my career, and I have Pat to thank for that. He was the guiding hand that got me started in the right direction. I didn't like it when the Flyers let him go, but he went on to have a great career in coaching with Los Angeles, Vancouver, Toronto, and Edmonton.

Pat Quinn left his mark on the coaching side of the game, and I was lucky enough to be there when the whole thing got off to such a great start.

Not many players were in the right place at the right time to have been both a teammate of as well as managed by a fellow named Robert Earle Clarke. In my book, you could substitute "winner" for Earle because that's what Bobby Clarke made not only of himself but almost everyone around him.

He hails from a small town, Flin Flon, in Manitoba, one province over from Saskatchewan, where I grew up, and so we had almost a built-in kinship right from the get-go. When I showed up in Philadelphia in 1979, Clarke had already been in the game for a decade and won two Stanley Cups and three MVP awards. At the outset, to say I was nervous just being near him would be an understatement. Thing is, he always tried his best to put the young guys at ease.

The first thing that struck me about him was his fantastic leadership qualities. He would take on whatever challenge was out there to win. You hear the expression "leads by example" about a lot of guys, but no one did it better than Clarkie. When it came to playing by the rules, he took it right to the limit. In that famous Summit Series with the Russians in 1972, he took out one of their best players, Valeri Kharlamov, with a whack to the lower leg after the Russian constantly badgered him with stickwork to the lower extremities. How far this crossed over the line remains to be seen, but you can be sure a lot of the hockey world was watching, most significantly his Flyers teammates back in Philadelphia. I always get a kick out of that famous quote by Clarke: "If I hadn't learned to lay on a two-hander once in a while, I'd never have left Flin Flon."

I was a pretty shy kid when I first hit the big time. In those first few years we had a lot of great leaders, including Clarke and later guys like Mark Howe, Dave Poulin, and Brad McCrimmon, so I was pretty quiet. I don't think I had the confidence to say a lot or offer my feelings on various hockey-related subjects, but after a couple years I adjusted and began to speak up a little bit more. I learned from Clarke and became more vocal.

In game action, we played the same way, both mindful that the defensive end of the rink was just as important as the offensive. Clarke always had to try a little harder because he wasn't a great skater. In practice, I was able to outwork him, but it was still an educational experience because he had this uncanny knack of always being in the right place at the right time. I would venture to say we learned things from each other. The intensity level in the practices was always high, especially during those first few years under Quinn, and that's where you gain mutual respect for one another.

Clarke's courage in the face of adversity was unquestioned. I heard a story about an incident that took place in the first round of the 1973 Stanley Cup playoffs. The Flyers were playing the old Minnesota North Stars, and Clarke was coming off a regular season in which he'd become the first player from an expansion team to register more than 100 points (104 on 37 goals, 67 assists). During the game, Bob was accidentally hit in the eye with an errant stick. The stickblade shattered a contact lens in his eye, and he was rushed to the hospital. Now a lot of players probably would have taken off a few games, because a scratched cornea is nothing to yawn about, but after pieces of the broken orb were removed from his eye, he was back in action for the very next game.

Having Clarke as a roommate at the World Championships in the early '80s offered me a chance to see up close and personal how a champion handles the pressure and demands of such a prestigious tournament. This isn't a time for fooling around. I was still in my early twenties and liked to have a good time. I was immature and went out a couple times and didn't really understand that you still have to play for your country. It goes without saying that expectation becomes even greater when you play for a hockey-crazed country like Canada. Clarke pulled me aside and asked me, did I want to be like one of the notorious drinkers on the Flyers or did I want to put everything I had into this experience and be proud of what I had achieved? It's easy to drink too much and be unable to perform. And believe me, there was some hard drinkers on those '70s Flyers teams. You should learn from that, Clarke said, and be a better player.

Clarke's words also came into play years later after I suffered the stroke. It goes without saying that my drinking days were over for good after my health crisis. I figured it was going to take some self-discipline to move away from drinking for good, but at the same time I wanted to make sure I left no stone unturned in my attempt to recover the best I could.

Social drinking is one thing; sitting in a room alone by yourself with a half-full bottle in front of you is something else. The latter is not in your best interests.

I did learn from that. After that 35-game unbeaten streak in 1979–80, the Flyers fell a bit on hard times, losing in the first round in 1982, 1983, and 1984. It got to be humiliating because after winning the first game in 1982 against the Rangers, we lost nine straight games over the next three years, including six to the Rangers and three more to the Capitals. I learned that I had to be much better in the playoffs. The level of play was definitely a notch higher than the regular season.

Clarke retired after the 1983–84 season and immediately became general manager of the Flyers. Things were going to be different, and the changes came in a hurry. Mike Keenan was hired as head coach, and the players responded. We would go on to make the Cup Final in two of the next three seasons, and I had some of my best seasons during this period. However, that group began to run out of gas by 1989 and some of the veterans were about to depart. I was one of them.

In the 1989–90 season, the Flyers were on course to miss the playoffs for the first time in 18 years. Just about everyone was deemed expendable. Clarke knew I wanted to play some meaningful hockey so he traded me to Boston, a move I loved. The Bruins were on their way to the NHL's best record and wound up getting home-ice advantage for the Stanley Cup playoffs, eventually won by Edmonton.

That season I had a pretty serious hand injury that cost me more than 25 games. When the season was over, I was in postseason action and Clarke was out of a job after 21 years as a Flyers employee. But as you may recall, we both ended up in Minnesota and it was a successful reunion, with the North Stars making the Final that year.

I would say Bob Clarke did more for me and my career than any person I've ever known, both on the ice and off it. I was just in the right place at the right time.

———————

It never hurts to have the best in the business serve as your mentor when you walk into a National Hockey League locker room for the first time. That's the circumstance I was fortunate enough to experience when I joined the Flyers in September 1979. Being a left wing, I knew that another left wing, Bill Barber, had been an instrumental part of the Flyers' two championships earlier in the decade. I wondered what kind of reception I would get, being this hotshot kid from junior hockey, but any fears I had were quickly laid to rest. Bill couldn't have been nicer.

I was a little bit in awe of Barber when I first met him. He had been playing on the LCB line with Reggie Leach and Bobby Clarke, one of the top units in NHL history. Clarke was one of the best passers to ever play the game, as his three MVP trophies will attest. Leach could snipe with the best of them. Bill was the perfect complement because he had this heavy shot that created all kinds of problems in front of opponents' nets. As if just stopping his shot weren't tough enough on goalies, Bill's accuracy was uncanny, even from long range. Maybe that's why he ended up scoring a franchise-record 420 goals.

There are so many other things I could add. He could play both sides of the ice and on the point for the power play because of that powerful slap shot. He was just so cool under pressure. He was consistent, scoring 20 or more goals in all 12 seasons he played in Philadelphia. His best work came in those two Stanley Cup years, plus the year after, when he posted 50 goals and 112 points. Defensively, he knew exactly how to position himself to thwart quick breaks. At times it was almost like having a third defenseman.

One of his most famous goals came in the 1976 Canada Cup when the final came down to the Canada crew and the team from Czechoslovakia. Bill scored a late goal to tie the score and Canada went on to win the championship in overtime.

Bill did some of his best work during the amazing 35-game unbeaten streak my first year. It seemed like there was a different first star every night, but you could make a case for "BB" being among the top five performers on a consistent basis. When we made a run to the Stanley Cup Final that year, Bill scored several pivotal goals against the New York Rangers and Minnesota North Stars.

It's no secret Bill would do whatever it took to win, including the occasional "dive." Back in the '70s, if he felt a stick hit his leg, he might lock his legs together and make a dramatic fall forward. Smart hockey. This was well before the days of today's minor penalties for embellishment. No doubt there were a few sly grins on the Flyers' bench when Bill got up and dusted himself off.

Fans at the old Spectrum loved watching him play because he had the long locks that would flow in the breeze whenever he reached top speed. Again, this was well before the days of mandatory helmets. It was kind of special just to see him flying around.

When I first started, Bill was really gracious with me. He kept telling me that "we needed someone like you." The advice was, *If you keep working hard and playing the game the right way, you will do well.*

On the power play, he could play anywhere on the ice. His shot really made the difference. A lot of those rockets hit other players' sticks and legs and wound up in the back of the net. It was the same thing with me. I had Tim Kerr to deflect the pucks all the time. Bill's shot was harder than mine. When it came to accuracy, he was second to none. More often than not, a goaltender would slightly shake his head in disbelief at the velocity of the puck that had just sailed by him.

As a team leader, Bill might have been underrated. He became captain of the team in the early '80s, when Clarke was an assistant coach, and the Flyers didn't miss a beat.

Bill was a lock for the Hockey Hall of Fame, a shrine into which he was inducted in 1990. The Flyers retired his No. 7 shortly after. Maybe he was overshadowed a bit by Clarke and goaltender Bernie Parent during the peak years, but I believe fans have come to appreciate him more as the years pass. Bill was forced to retire in 1985 after undergoing major reconstructive knee surgery. At that point, he not only led the franchise in regular season goals but was tied with Rick MacLeish for the most playoff goals (53) in team history.

After he retired from playing, Bill went into coaching. He started in the minors, first briefly with the Hershey Bears in 1985 and later, after serving as a Flyers assistant coach, with the AHL Philadelphia Phantoms (the Flyers' farm team), where he won the Calder Cup in 1998. When he took over behind the Flyers' bench in late 2000, I was working in the radio booth and calling the team's games. It was impressive to see him win the Jack Adams Award for NHL coach of the year in 2000–01.

From there, Bill signed on with the Tampa Bay Lightning as their director of player personnel for a number of years. That's how his name wound up on the Stanley Cup again in 2004. He returned to Philly in 2008 as a scouting consultant, and his sharp eye for evaluating talent remains vital to this day.

He really knows what makes the game tick, even a half century after he first started playing. He and Clarke live near each other in Sarasota, Florida, so I'm sure there are plenty of reunions to converse about today's game and what it was like in yesteryear. For Bill, it's been a pretty amazing career. He and I talk all the time. I take photographs, and he's always gracious. Just what you would expect from a hockey icon.

I was working in the Flyers' radio booth the afternoon of December 8, 2001, when we learned Bill's wife, Jenny, had passed away from lung cancer. Bill was coaching the Flyers at that time and, following advice from his family, decided to work behind the bench that afternoon for a home game against the Minnesota Wild.

The players were not even aware of Jenny's passing until right before the game. One player said the stress level in the Barber family household must have been very high, and Bill's only release, other than having his children around, was coming to the rink. Somehow Bill stayed focused on the game at hand. But it could not have been easy. Bill is well-liked by everyone, and it must have been tough to go through such an ordeal.

CHAPTER 5

PUT ME IN, COACH

IN HOCKEY, LIKE OTHER SPORTS, it's all about being in the right place at the right time. Personally, when it came to the coaches I played for in my 15-year NHL career, I couldn't have been more fortunate. Look at some of the names: Quinn, Keenan, Holmgren, Gainey. Come to think of it, back in their prime as players, they would have made up a pretty good nucleus of a Stanley Cup–contending team, although Mike Keenan probably would have been better positioned behind the bench calling the shots for that group.

The Flyers were pretty much a contending team throughout the '70s, including their two championships. When I came on board, Pat Quinn was running the show and, from what I recall, his practices were pretty long—like 90 minutes. Pat wanted to do everything, and I mean everything, to make sure there was no indecision. We worked on breakouts until the cows came home. The Flyers' power play was pretty lethal, and a lot of the credit for that goes to how long we rehearsed it from all different angles. We seemed to do that with all special teams. And the drills paid off. To wit—in Game 3 of the 1980 semifinals vs. Minnesota, Bill Barber scored four goals, including one on the power play and one shorthanded in a 5–3 win at the old Met Center.

I didn't mind the lengthy practices because I was a rookie, we had great leaders, and we didn't lose a game (that 35-game unbeaten streak) for the better part of three months. So, you dealt with it and at the end of the day, the players were better off for it because they really improved their conditioning level.

When Keenan showed up in 1984, no one really knew what to think. We knew he had won championships at the college and minor league levels, but his tactics were still a bit of a mystery. Keenan had fast-paced practices, maybe just 45 minutes in length, and he expected you to keep up. This coach liked to work on the power play before practice even officially began. Just a 10-minute refresher course got the job done. There was very little nonsense or kidding around when "Iron Mike" had the whistle around his neck. Some players might not have liked his approach, but after we went to the Stanley Cup Final in his first NHL season, they had to respect it.

This coach knew how to get the best out of his players, and he really worked his magic with young guys like Rick Tocchet, Peter Zezel, Scott Mellanby, and Derrick Smith. These youngsters were a big part of our success during Keenan's reign.

Before we move on, the debate regarding whether Keenan should be in the Hockey Hall of Fame should be addressed. Keenan's only Stanley Cup came with the New York Rangers in 1994 (ending a 54-year franchise drought), but he took the Flyers to the last round twice and the Chicago Blackhawks once. Critics will say his winning percentage (.555) wasn't high enough or that he burned too many bridges along the way. But if I had a vote, it would be cast in his favor for the Toronto shrine.

And I bet if you took a poll of general managers, coaches, and players from that era, a majority of them would agree with me that Keenan is qualified for the Hall and would vote for him if they were on the selection committee. He began pro coaching with the Buffalo Sabres–owned Rochester Americans and won an AHL title with them. Scotty Bowman was in the Buffalo organization at the time and no doubt the nine-time Stanley Cup championship coach had some influence on Keenan's budding career at the time.

A somewhat humorous story: One time during a Flyers Stanley Cup playoff run, a bunch of out-of-town writers got Keenan in his office after a practice at the Flyers' rink. One guy got confused and addressed the coach as "Larry," mixing up the name with a former Flyer player. Keenan didn't blink an eye and proceeded to answer questions for the next five minutes. Then, as the writers were filing out of his office, Keenan stood up and in a raised voice barked, "And it's Mike, not Larry…"

When Keenan was let go after the 1987–88 season, the Flyers brought in Paul Holmgren to coach the team. Holmgren was known as a stand-up guy as a player and one who was young enough to identify with a lot of the players. He had been Keenan's assistant coach after retiring as a player and incorporated some of Keenan's approaches into his own. Having GM Bob Clarke as a personal friend didn't hurt either. In Holmgren's first year, the Flyers made it to the semifinals before bowing to Montreal. The following season, the Flyers would miss the playoffs for the first time since 1972.

Holmgren made the best of a tough situation. Talent-wise, the Flyers were in a transitional period. Star players such as Tim Kerr, Mark Howe, Dave Poulin, and even myself were starting to lose a step. Change was in the wind.

A few words here about my brief stay in Boston at the tail end of the 1989–90 season. My contract was running out and I figured I was only going to spend a few months there. The controversial Mike Milbury was running the show. He ran the standard one-hour practice with an All-Star cast, including Ray Bourque, Cam Neely, and Poulin. I was new to the roster and Milbury had his favorites, so I didn't get as much ice time as I thought I would. But I just decided to put up with it.

When Clarke showed up in the Twin Cities, it wasn't all that surprising that I wound up there, too. The legendary Bobby Smith was the centerpiece of the club and I think we caught some people by surprise. Bob Gainey wanted longer practices, too, which made sense since he always paid attention to details as a player. One thing that bothered me was a constant practicing of the infamous "left-wing lock," a form of defense in which you try to funnel everything to one side of the rink to limit the offensive options. I didn't like it because I was a left wing and I wanted to force the action all the time. But I was the kind of guy who followed orders, so I put up with it.

As I've stated, the last year or two of my career was focused on getting to the 1,000-point and 1,000-game milestones, when I decided to give it one more shot with the Hartford Whalers after my stopover in Minnesota.

It wasn't a very deep or talented roster, but it did have Sean Burke in goal, young defenseman Chris Pronger, and veteran backliner Brad McCrimmon on it. That year, we weren't doing very well, and GM Holmgren decided to step aside and appoint Pierre Maguire as the new head coach. That was better for me because he played me a little bit more and I got some additional power-play time. That's when I got my thousand games and points. Otherwise I might not have gotten to those milestones.

Holmgren the player was someone who I really learned from. We were on that 1980 team together and then a few seasons after that. He said he learned his competitiveness from Clarke. Both Clarke and some of the other vets on the Flyers showed him how to be a good coach. Holmgren was a lot like Craig Berube in that they learned to figure things out, and no doubt that helped Berube guide the St. Louis Blues to their first Stanley

Cup. Berube learned how to communicate with some of the team's better players.

And I might add another fellow who picks up all the details of the game quite well is Rick Tocchet, who became head coach of the Vancouver Canucks in 2023. "Toc" knows the game inside and out. I know they didn't have good teams in his two previous stops at Tampa Bay and Arizona. But it was a good experience for a guy that I call a friend. He's learning how to communicate with players, and that's half the battle.

———————

If you're going to take pro hockey seriously, you can't be too serious about your nightlife on the road. Oh, there are plenty of opportunities and lots of hours to kill, but the best use of that time is probably not spent in bars or flirting in some hotel lobby.

In the '80s, we did have our share of *bon vivants*. Certain cities afforded athletes better chances than others. Guys like the late Peter Zezel did his share of night patrol, and others, like my pal Brad McCrimmon and Derrick Smith, knew how to have a good time.

These guys would go out for a few beers and check out the women patrons. Brad was the worst because he saw the whole thing as a big challenge. He was a fun guy to hang out with. When all was said and done, it was pretty tame stuff. In all candor, not many guys challenged curfew.

A lot of our home practices were on Fridays, either late mornings or early afternoons because we played a lot of games on Thursday nights and then one of the weekend nights. In those days, Sunday night home games were a staple. If the Friday practice was in the morning, a bunch of us would get together for lunch at the Philadium over on Packer Avenue. It wasn't uncommon to have a couple beers and a sandwich. The place was usually full of Flyers fans and a lot of them knew they might get a glimpse of one of their favorite players or even enjoy a short chat.

Getting from city to city by air travel was more than just a small challenge. We always flew commercial. This created a few uncomfortable situations, like the 6'6" Kjell Samuelsson crammed into the middle segment of a three-seater. He'd be stuck and more than a little uncomfortable. This is where someone of slightly smaller stature like me had a much easier time of it.

The idle time at airports led to some rather creative pranks. Some of them were as old as the hills, like poking a hole in a dollar bill (probably a $10 bill now), attaching a string to it (fishing line worked best because it was not as easy to detect), and then tossing the contraption into the busy walkway traversing boarding areas. We would watch with glee as people eyed the money lying on the floor. They would reach down to grab it only to have it yanked away. We got a lot of laughs with that one. It's a spoof that's as old as a redwood tree, but it still evokes some hearty chuckles.

We had our share of comedians on the flights, too. Goaltender Bob Froese could imitate a crying baby—*Wa-a-a-a!*—from the back seats so well that people would be turning their heads to see how distressed the little tyke really was. Some of the Flyers would be cracking up.

In my opinion, there's nothing quite like French food, and that's why Montreal had such appeal to me. One of the highlights of a visit there was a stroll through the old city where you could go to a place like Gibbys for dinner. People usually were all dressed up and it had a real cosmopolitan feel to it.

For pure hockey atmosphere, you just couldn't do better than a Saturday night game at the old Montreal Forum. That's where they had replicas of a world-best 24 Stanley Cups on display.

Right up there with the palace in Quebec was the old Chicago Stadium, which was home to the Blackhawks from 1929 to 1994. What a place. The organist and his world-famous keyboard could belt out the classics like no other venue in the good old NHL. We would set up shop at the classic Drake Hotel and more than a few embellishments were exchanged in late-night conversations.

The most vivid memory I have from those days is that they had a famous singer perform "The Star-Spangled Banner" before games. Fans would stand and sing and clap through the whole song. That got everyone in a competitive frame of mind. They would always complete those last few notes of the national anthem with a loud flourish. The cheers were deafening, and everyone was surely having a good time.

Now any Canadian who tells you he doesn't appreciate an occasional break to get into some warm weather in the middle of winter probably is telling an old-fashioned fib. I'll admit I really enjoyed our occasional visit to Los Angeles to play the Kings. I would pack a few pairs of shorts because I knew we would probably have a couple days off, especially when the trip fell during Christmas week. Some of us even ventured down to San Diego, where there were some beautiful beaches. Even an occasional round of golf wasn't out of the question. To be honest, I don't know how the Kings kept their minds on their profession with so many distractions. Maybe the novelty eventually just gets taken for granted.

There were plenty of stories to tell, none more bizarre than the sudden disappearance of one of our favorite dive bars, an old place. We were in there one night and the next day we found out it had burned down. We laughed and thought one of our players, Dennis Ververgaert, might have carelessly lit one of his cigarettes and that was the culprit.

In just about every professional sport, the debate will never die: Is today's game as good as—or better than—what was played 10, 20, 50 years ago? Every generation has its own opinion. Those who have lived through the NHL's expansion from six to 12 teams in 1967 and then eventually 32 teams by 2023–24 know the controversy most likely will never be settled.

Veteran observers will admit today's players are, for the most part, bigger and stronger and faster than the old days. The best skaters can make it from one end of the rink to the other in almost, literally, the blink of an eye. Whether that makes for a more entertaining game remains to be seen. Maybe it's just me, but when we played in the 1980s, players seemed to be a little more creative with the puck.

To me, today's game isn't quite as exciting as a generation or two ago. Compared to when the Broad Street Bullies and other hockey team's tough guys played, there isn't as much hitting anymore. The defense forces the play all the time, which ultimately reduces the number of quality scoring chances. In the games that I've watched, play can go on for four or five minutes at a time without a whistle. Plus, they used to have a no two-line pass rule regarding the red line, so that opens up the game a little bit more. That rule is gone, and some might see that as a step forward, but it might make teams a little more cautious on the defensive side of the puck.

They call so many penalties now that it does have an impact on the game. Fighting has been greatly reduced, so you don't see as many majors. In the '80s, it wasn't unusual to see the game stopped two or three times a night if the teams really didn't like each other or if two opposing players had a beef with one another. Coaches will tell you that the momentum of a game can change with a good brawl and bench leaders such as Fred Shero and Mike Keenan had that option in their toolbox.

Technology and so forth also changed the game. Sticks went from wood to lightweight synthetic materials. Goalie pads got bigger. Finally, they had to put some rules in there. Remember when the Flyers' Garth Snow skated out for the 1997 Cup Final against Detroit looking like RoboCop? One scribe asked if he had the late Jimmy Hoffa, the famous teamster boss, buried under one of his bulging shoulder pads. In the earlier years, you had more open space at which to shoot.

Smarter players can create space for others. Once the whistle blows for a penalty, their brains are whirling. They're trying to figure out how they're going to exploit the four-man defender unit, be it through quick passing or creating havoc in front of the net. If you watch closely, the brighter guys either move the puck quickly or find open space for the best shooting angles. We had Peter Zezel and Pelle Eklund as setup guys for sharpshooters like Tim Kerr and me. Also, on the power play, the point man is important, and we had one of the best with Mark Howe. They even put me on the point for three or four years because I was known for having a quick release. All I had to do was get the puck on net, and I knew Timmy was somewhere down there scrounging around for rebounds.

By 1990 I was with the Bruins. Ray Bourque at point could bring it with the best of them. I figured that out soon enough and stationed myself right where I thought a rebound might come. The puck movement was second to none. In fact, the puck moved so quickly some fans had a hard time keeping up with the back-and-forth flow. They set it up so well, it was like a work of art.

With the North Stars, it was more of the same. Bobby Smith was at the center of it all, and Neal Broten was the quarterback for the power play. Mike Modano and I were in front, looking to hawk the puck if it came off the goalie's equipment. That year, 1991, all eight of my goals were power-play goals in the playoffs and that was a record that will never be broken because the North Stars don't exist anymore.

Getting back to the debate, there's no question about the skill level of today's game. There are moves made that simply didn't happen a generation back. But the lack of creativity, as I see it, is the puck gets dumped in and then it gets dumped out. The smarter players hang on to the puck and wait to see what their options are. I'm not sure today's game is as exciting as the one we had. You probably won't see another Wayne Gretzky, Mario Lemieux, Jaromír Jágr, or Mark Messier anymore, because the style of today's game just simply won't allow it. While the players are quicker and most likely better conditioned, the game, to me, just isn't quite as exciting. I guess to each his own.

CHAPTER 6

BEST OF THE BEST

Winning the Stanley Cup on this side of the pond is a very big deal to Canada and the United States because, for those countries, it symbolizes world hockey supremacy.

Yet in the other corners of the globe, there have been other prizes with just as much—or perhaps even more—prestige.

Since the Winter Olympics opened to professional players at Nagano in 1998, that competition has been viewed by many as the ultimate because of the strong feelings of nationalism. Because it includes teams from all around the globe and now involves play-for-pay competitors, there is no need for asterisks. The same could be said for other past international tournaments, such as the annual World Championships and former events like the World Cup and the Canada Cup.

Now that I mention it, the 1987 Canada Cup quickly comes to mind—not only because my native country won it but because of the powerful field and the number of superstars in it.

Heck, on my line alone there were two of the best players ever to lace on a pair of skates—Wayne Gretzky and Mario Lemieux. To have played with such hockey royalty was indeed an honor.

Any real success I enjoyed in these global events didn't come easy. The Flyers weren't exactly setting the world on fire during the early '80s.

After the amazing run to the final round of 1980, it seemed like the old guard from the 1970s was beginning to lose a bit of competitive steam. Injuries were starting to catch up to some of the stars from what was left of those championship teams in 1974 and 1975. We didn't get too far in the postseason from 1981 to 1984. We were still competitive in the regular season but, without a goaltender such as Bernie Parent (forced to retire in 1979 due to injury) and with some instability behind the bench (Pat Quinn and Bob McCammon switched places a couple times), it just wasn't quite the same as the previous decade.

So it was so good just to play with Team Canada. After the Flyers went out early, I had a chance to keep my hockey year going by joining my nation's team at the World Championships. In 1982, the World Championships were held in Helsinki, Finland. Coincidentally, Bob Clarke was my roommate over there in Scandinavia. And I had a chance to hang out with another veteran, Curt Giles of the Minnesota North Stars. It was my first crack at serious international play, and I really didn't know any better. I just went out and played.

At night I would join up with a bunch of guys and party a little bit. I wasn't taking the whole thing too seriously; not much more than you would expect from a single 23-year-old. Well, that sort of behavior didn't last too long. Clarke came up to me one day with a rather serious expression on his face. We talked, and that's when I realized I had to make sure I was playing my very best hockey even at the World Championships because I was a representative of Team Canada. Czechoslovakia and the Soviet Union met in the gold medal game, and we settled for the bronze. Gretzky was a big part of that moral victory. There was some consolation in at least being on the podium and bringing home some kind of medal.

I learned a lot from that experience, and it helped prepare me for the next World Championships in 1983. This time the competition was in Munich, Germany. I hung out with Michel Goulet, the former Quebec Nordique who was inducted into the Hockey Hall of Fame in 1998. In my mind, he was one of the best left wings in the history of the game. Scoring 50 or more goals in four consecutive years pretty much confirmed that. At this tournament I found out you had to lift your game because you were playing against the very best the game had to offer. I figured out that I had to take this tournament more seriously—no more nights out on the town. That's because I was still representing Team Canada and all it stood for. Canada takes pride in being at the very peak of the sport and no one who plays for the maple leaf flag wants to diminish that reputation.

In the 1983 tournament, my production picked up. I had four goals and four assists in 10 games. Again, a lot of Canada's best players were still involved in Stanley Cup competition but somehow, we were good enough to win the bronze medal for a second consecutive year. This was a good learning experience for me. I always took pride in playing for Team Canada. Even when I was playing in Canadian junior hockey, I looked forward to competing internationally against guys at or near my age. It became apparent that tournaments like the Spengler Cup carried almost as much prestige as the other competitions. I was proud just to be a part of that. You were playing with and against some of the best players in the world.

Finally, in 1987, all the experience paid off for me and my fellow Team Canada brethren at the Canada Cup, which was held in late summer prior to the start of the 1987–88 NHL season. The tournament included some of the best players ever to have competed in hockey. The Flyers were coming off a run all the way to Game 7 in the Stanley Cup Final against the Edmonton Oilers, and I just happened to lead Philly in scoring, setting a record in the process. I was very proud of that.

Everything was aligned properly for me personally. My Flyers coach, Mike Keenan, was behind Team Canada's bench, and Bob Clarke, the Flyers' GM, was running the show. There was no break after the Stanley Cup Final ended because Canada Cup training camp started right after that. It was special for me, because I was right about at the peak of my career. People were finally acknowledging that I was one of the best players in the game. This was another chance to play on the same line with Gretzky and Lemieux all through the tournament. I felt really comfortable because some of my teammates, like Rick Tocchet and Doug Crossman, were also on the Canada roster.

Rookie Flyers goaltender Ron Hextall was also on the squad. He was only a backup to Stanley Cup champion netminder Grant Fuhr, but even though he wasn't playing, he was a big part of the team. Ultimately, it wound up being one of the best tournaments ever.

That championship best-of-three against the Soviet Union was as good as anything the world has seen, including the Olympics and the Stanley Cup. The hockey was faster; every decision was a split-second judgment. The Russians had their best players, and this was before defection was allowed, so none of their players had competed in the NHL just yet. The first Russians weren't allowed into the NHL draft until 1988. Some of the names are easily recognizable: Viacheslav Fetisov, Igor Kravchuk, Andrei Lomakin, Igor Larionov, Alexander Semak, Sergei Nemchinov, Vladimir Krutov, Sergei Makarov, and Dmitri Bykov.

But the Canada lineup wasn't too shabby either. We had Wayne Gretzky, Mario Lemieux, Grant Fuhr, Mark Messier, Dale

Hawerchuk, Glenn Anderson, and Brent Sutter, along with Doug Gilmour, Paul Coffey, and Ray Bourque. In all, 12 future Hall of Famers.

A lot of the Russians played for their team year-round. They were in this tournament to win it. It was best-of-three, and the outcomes couldn't have been closer. We lost the first game in over-time. We won the second game in Hamilton, Ontario, in double overtime. I was on the ice for the winning goal—in fact, I was the one who passed the puck to Lemieux for the score.

It all came down to Game 3. There was a lot on the line—things were changing in the world; the Berlin Wall would fall two years later, in 1989. Soon the Soviet Union as we knew it would be no more.

The game didn't start off so well for us at Copps Coliseum in Hamilton. In fact, we were down 3–0 before a lot of fans had reached their seats. It was a bit of a shock for experienced play-ers such as Messier and Hawerchuk. Then we started to make a comeback, and it was just unbelievable hockey. That was saying something, because the Russians had a great team. Being down three goals less than 10 minutes into the game looked like an insurmountable hill to climb. I thought to myself, *Oh, boy!*

But Keenan was up to his old tricks and decided to change his lines around. I wound up on a line with Tocchet and Sutter. Amazingly, Tocchet scored and then I scored. Soon the score was tied. It went back and forth, and you really couldn't guess who was going to win. We were up 5–4 after two periods. Russia tied it and it stayed 5–5 until the closing minutes. Then with less than two minutes to play, Keenan sent Gretzky, Lemieux, and Hawerchuk out for a faceoff in Canada's zone. Hawerchuk won the faceoff and Gretzky, Lemieux, and Larry Murphy raced up the ice. Gretzky dropped a pass to Lemieux, who fired the puck past goalie Sergei Mylnikov with 1:26 left on the clock. You should have seen our players leap off the bench in unison like we had just won the Stanley Cup in sudden-death overtime.

It's considered one of the most memorable plays in Canadian sports history.

That Russian team was about as good as they come. At this point, Russia was still known as the Soviet Union and players from that country had not yet played in the NHL. So, despite all their success in the Winter Olympics, no one was really sure how good they were, although they had taken Canada to the limit in the 1972 Summit Series and the Flyers were the only team to beat them in their 1976 North American tour.

Consider this: within two years, the entire Soviet top forward unit of Sergei Makarov, Igor Larionov, and Vladimir Krutov, plus the No. 1 defense pairing of Slava Fetisov and Alexei Kasatonov, would be playing in the NHL.

You have to remember that this Cold War of hockey might never happen again. There was a lot of international prestige at stake, and the NHL's two best players, Gretzky and Lemieux, along with a strong supporting cast, were up to the challenge. There were times on the bench when I was like a fan, mesmerized by the speed and skill unfolding in front of me.

It was a memorable moment in my career. I was part of something that was the best in the world. I was beginning to wonder after my Flyers teams came up short in the 1980, 1985, and 1987 Stanley Cup Finals. I not only won the gold medal but was a big part of it, having played with Gretzky and Lemieux for most of the tournament. I was able to show a different side of myself as a player—I checked hard and made sure that I was back to help on the defensive side of things. It was really special to play with a couple of immortals. I got to know them a little bit more after the tournament, and we still talk often.

CHAPTER 7

STAR LIGHT, STAR BRIGHT

A S GRATIFYING AS IT IS for a professional player to enjoy team success throughout their career, there's nothing like an NHL All-Star Game or two to validate one's tenure in the big show.

I was fortunate enough to play in five of them, including the memorable 1990 midseason classic in Pittsburgh. Of all the games I either played in or witnessed, the one held at the "Igloo," aka the Civic Arena in Pittsburgh, on January 21 had to be the most memorable.

This one will be remembered for a lot of things, like Penguins superstar Mario Lemieux scoring four goals, three of them on his very first three shots in the first period. I set him up for his first goal just 21 seconds into the game, and the place was going crazy. There were plenty of legendary players in this game featuring the home team Wales Conference stars against those of the Campbell Conference.

This game was originally scheduled to be played in Montreal but because Rendez-Vous '87 was played just down the road in Quebec City, the NHL asked (mandated?) that the '90 All-Star Game be moved to Pittsburgh, which was originally scheduled to host the game in 1993.

This All-Star weekend featured the addition of the Heroes of Hockey game between past NHL greats. The All-Star Skills

Competition, a competition between the players invited to the All-Star Game, also originated here.

One of the other big changes was the move from the traditional Tuesday night scheduling to Sunday afternoon. This allowed NBC to air the game live in the U.S.—bringing Wayne Gretzky and Lemieux to a national audience for the first time. The two head coaches, referees, and other officials wore microphones to pick up more of the behind-the-scenes action. And for the first time, NBC was allowed to conduct interviews with players during stoppages in play. A lot of these changes were later incorporated into the regular season and postseason games.

I was hurt much of that season. I had been traded from the Flyers to Boston and only managed to play a total of 54 games split between the two teams. I think because of the playoff perfor-mance I had the year before (14 goals in 18 games), I got voted into the All-Star Game. Sometimes stuff like that gets overlooked, so it was nice to know that someone was paying attention. I was getting older by now and a little more mature. It was nice to get a last shot playing with Lemieux in this environment.

After Mario's performance, the thing I probably remember most about that game was my mission to stop Gretzky at any cost. I checked him like crazy throughout the game. He failed to get a single point, which was kind of amazing. I was pretty proud of myself. Mario was the MVP of the game and won the car. He was such a great player to be around in All-Star Games. Especially that last one in Pittsburgh, where he was a hometown hero. I remember talking with Brett Hull and a couple other players at the dinner. It was very special for me because this was probably going to be my last All-Star Game.

One sobering note was a bus ride one morning in which Montreal defenseman Chris Chelios and I were in the same gen-eral proximity. Chelios was the player who had sent me to the hospital during a game in the 1989 Eastern Conference semifinals. I was knocked unconscious but only missed one game. However, not a lot of time had passed since that incident, so the energy between the two of us was still a bit negative. We didn't talk. It felt a little different—we were still mad at each other for what happened with my concussion. I didn't want to talk with him about that.

Otherwise it was a good time for me. The last one was special because, with more teams and fewer players from each one, it was harder to earn a selection. So I was pretty proud of this one.

The 1980 All-Star Game was the first I played in and probably my second-favorite of the big five. The Flyers had seven players on the team. Besides myself, there were Bill Barber, Rick MacLeish, Reggie Leach, Pete Peeters, Norm Barnes, and Jimmy Watson. This tilt was played at the brand-new Joe Louis Arena, home of the Detroit Red Wings in downtown Detroit. I was a rookie and a bit starstruck (pardon the pun). Gordie Howe, still playing for the Hartford Whalers at the tender age of 51, got a huge ovation.

I played on a line with my Flyers teammate Reggie Leach along with New York's Phil Esposito. What an amazing experience for a 21-year-old. Having so many Flyers on the team made for not only a comfortable experience but a memorable one as well.

In my opinion, this was an era when players still really tried to make it seem like the outcome mattered. Maybe there was some pride involved: East vs. West and that sort of thing. It's not like today, when there doesn't seem to be any sense of urgency and no one wants to watch it. Back in the day, players still wanted to win. If you won the game, you got a ring or some other such trinket for winning the game. I remember the night before the 1980 game we were out partying with a bunch of guys from our conference, guys like the Islanders' Mike Bossy, Bryan Trottier, and Clark Gillies. Now, those New York boys (by way of Canada) knew

how to party. Game the next night? No big deal. Nobody seemed
to care. It was an NHL All-Star Game; everybody just had some
beer on the eve of the game and had some fun with it. Oh, the
stories that were told! I did a lot of listening and a lot of grinning.

The whole experience was pretty amazing. I'll never forget
playing against Ol' Gordie. I had a goal and an assist. The goal
came early in the third period to give the Campbell Conference a
3–2 lead. But then the Wales Conference rattled off four straight
goals for a 6–3 win. Howe, playing in his 23rd and final All-Star
Game, assisted on the last goal. What a way to end an All-Star
career!

Then came my selection to the 1982 NHL All-Star Game. By
then I was a bit more established in the league. I was getting a
lot of power-play time and playing on the Rat Patrol line back
in Philly with Kenny "the Rat" Linseman and Paul Holmgren.
Having played in the 1980 game, I knew what to expect in 1982
at Washington. They had a big dinner at the White House. I had
a chance to meet President Ronald Reagan. I had to get a couple
photographs with him and that was real special for me. Barber and
I were the only two Flyers in the game. It was fairly close by, so
the two of us just jumped in a car and drove there. In hindsight,
one of the highlights of the trip was getting to meet President
Reagan. I still have his photograph on my office wall.

The 1984 game at New Jersey was special for me because the
only two Flyers on the team were myself and Tim Kerr. It seemed
like Tim and I had good chemistry. He was a scoring machine. He
put together four straight 50-or-more-goal seasons between 1983
and 1987. In the 1985 playoffs, Tim scored a record four goals
in a span of just a little over eight minutes at Madison Square
Garden to help beat the New York Rangers 6–5. The '84 All-Star
Game was played at what was then Brendan Byrne Arena in the

Meadowlands. Like Washington, getting to the game in New Jersey did not require a plane flight so we just drove there by car.

Our Wales Conference team jumped out to a 5–0 lead in the first period and maybe we fell asleep a little bit in the third period because a 7–3 lead quickly dissolved into a 7–6 nail-biter. Gretzky & Co. put on some real pressure, but we hung on for the win.

Next came the 1986 game in Hartford, Connecticut. Again, I was on a line with Kerr and this time Flyers teammate Dave Poulin at center. I scored a couple goals in the Wales Conference's 4–3 win over the Campbell Conference and thought I might have a shot at the game MVP and the new car that went with it. But Campbell goaltender Grant Fuhr really played well in the loss and the honor went to him. I couldn't complain. Playing with all the best players in the world again was a great experience. A couple of goals made it feel like I was one of the game's best players.

When you get to play alongside some of the best players in the world, there's a certain feeling of satisfaction that you've made it all the way to the top. Also, getting put into crucial situations, even in an All-Star Game, generally means you're trustworthy at both ends of the rink.

I'll admit I was all eyes and ears at a few of these games. I wanted to study how some of the game's best players reacted in certain situations. Yes, you see them in regular season action, but these All-Star Games were almost pure skill with almost no checking. It was just interesting to see how certain players performed in open-ice situations.

Besides that, you're in the same locker room with these guys and you get a chance to talk as if you really were teammates. It's an interesting dynamic and something that stayed with me long after my career ended.

CHAPTER 8

THE DYNAMIC DUO

I F THERE WAS EVER a case to be made for using the tags "1" and "1A" it would have to be for designating the two best players of their generation, Wayne Gretzky and Mario Lemieux.

Oh, you could debate the merits of players from a bygone era, such as Gordie Howe, Bobby Hull, Rocket Richard, or Bobby Orr. But with the exception of playing against Howe in 1980 when he was 51 years old, the others I only saw on television or watched on videotape.

I had the good fortune of seeing these two modern icons from both sides of the puck—playing against Gretzky in his peak years with the high-powered Edmonton Oilers and Lemieux at the height of his power with the Pittsburgh Penguins—and with both all-timers at international tournaments such as the 1987 Canada Cup.

While Gretzky's goal total of 894 has stood as the NHL's all-time best since 1999, it's his ability to pass the puck that has always impressed me. Now that certainly isn't breaking any news with your average hockey fan beyond the age of 35. Everyone watched "the Great One" make these radar-accurate setups as if he had eyes in the back of his head. His penchant for finding the open shooter was uncanny. He would put on a burst of speed to get across the blue line, then slam on the brakes, and this gave him that extra split second of time to find the open man.

One thing that impressed me about Gretzky was the way he handled his fame right off the bat—that is, his relationship with the media. Some guys might have been intimidated by so much attention, but Wayne learned to get out in front of it. It was like he anticipated the questions that were coming and was ready for them.

Lemieux took a little longer to reach a comfort level because when he was drafted in 1984, he mostly spoke French. So it took him a while, maybe five years or so, until he looked a little more at ease.

To me, they had talent that was clearly above the rest of the NHL players. You might see a Mark Messier or a Jaromír Jágr make the occasional sensational play, but not on an almost nightly basis like Wayne or Mario.

Gretzky enjoyed early success, but the Oilers had some great players, such as Messier and Jari Kurri. These guys played in the wild, wild West and they thought nothing of running up the score. How do you think Wayne got to 215 points in one season? That might be a record that's never broken, unless the league makes some radical rule changes. I wanted people to know that Gretzky never gave up.

I was on the ice at Edmonton on the night of December 30, 1981, for one of the most incredible feats in hockey history. Wayne lit up the Flyers for five goals to reach the 50 mark in just 39 games. In fact, he scored a total of nine goals in two games to reach this lofty plateau. To my way of thinking, the 50 in 39 will stand the test of time, or should I say a long time. That's the year he posted 212 points.

Even when he reached that amazing total of 215 (which may never be broken), Wayne's attitude toward the people who played the game and the fans who watched it never really changed. He made himself approachable when he was in public, gave generous interviews when afforded the time, and did his best to credit his teammates whenever the occasion called for it. There were instances almost every night when he could have taken credit for a positive development, but dominating the spotlight just wasn't in his personality.

On the ice, Wayne was always thinking of a move or two ahead. Like an elite pocket billiards player, he was always interested in what would happen if he chose Option A or Option B. What would be the outcome of making a pass instead of taking what would seem like an obvious shot? No doubt he watched an opponent intently while recovering on the bench in between shifts. On the power play, it was almost like having another coach on the ice. If there was a way to exploit an opponent, you could be sure Wayne would find a way to do it.

Wayne just always wanted to keep on scoring, which certainly gave hometown fans something to always cheer about. Even if the game was out of reach, he had his eye on the net. There was just something about him—he never seemed to be quite satisfied with his performance. Well, maybe that five-goal game.

Keep in mind, the Oilers didn't exactly play in a powerhouse division in those days. The hockey was pretty wide-open, like the game back in 1981 that ended in a 7–5 score in favor of the Oilers. Come to think of it, hockey was pretty wide-open in both conferences back in the '80s. Wayne had a powerful shot, which was accurate and often came off the tail end of a good old-fashioned deke.

One thing he was known for was setting up behind the net, and it drove opposing forwards like me almost to the point of distraction because he was so good at finding the open man out front. And if he managed to get the goalies to glance over his shoulder to see which way the play was going, Wayne would simply go the other way. He would thread a pinpoint pass to a guy like Kurri for a one-timer, which seldom missed its target. It was pretty amazing stuff. Teams would try different things to defend that arrangement, and nothing seemed to work.

Then there were the two-on-one rushes. Because of his skating, he drew people to him, then he passed to an open man and the goalie was a sitting duck. Teams would review miles of videotape, but it didn't seem to help. When you went this way, Wayne went that way.

Lemieux was more of a scoring machine with a nose for the net. At 6'4", he enjoyed an incredible wingspan, which allowed him to speed the puck around defenders while protecting it in a cradle move. They don't get any smoother than Mario. Once I saw him basically deke his way around four, maybe all five, defenders and then put the puck in the net. All you could do is slowly shake your head and give it that sheepish grin.

One of the great things about Mario was his balance on his skates. He had an incredible base, which made him so hard to bodycheck off the puck. At times it was like man against boys. His shot was the stuff of legend. In the '87 Canada Cup, he was going top shelf all the time, which is what gets fans *oohing* and *aahing*. When Wayne and Mario played on the same line in the '87 Canada Cup it was something to behold. Fans certainly got their money's worth. It was fun to watch them work together, even if it was only for a few games. They were so in sync, one would never guess they played on opposing teams in the NHL.

When you think about it, I believe Mario—who was in his early twenties at the time—really learned from the leaders at that Canada Cup. He learned how to win, which might sound simple but it's true. You have to excel at all aspects of the game and that's where "Super Mario" really put it together. Before that, when we played him, our Ron Sutter would dog him all the time. But after some time, No. 66 figured out how to operate even with a shadow on him and his game picked up after that. Once the '90s rolled around, he had Tocchet, Kevin Stevens, Mark Recchi, Jágr, and others to lighten the offensive responsibilities. He would let them take on some of the scoring responsibilities but when the Penguins needed a big goal, Mario was still the man.

He was so good because he played in a tougher division against gritty teams like the Flyers, Devils, Capitals, and Rangers. It was a little tougher for him to score but he still was awesome. He always seemed to find a way. Most impressive—he battled through cancer and kept on going. His courage was an inspiration to every hockey fan, whether they were in Pittsburgh or anywhere else around North America.

So looking back, it was pretty amazing for me to be on the same rink with these guys. In my book, they're right up there with the legends of any era.

What is a clutch player?

Webster's Dictionary defines the term as someone who is "dependable in crucial situations." Well, over the course of my playing career, I ran into a bunch of those—either on my side of the ice or someone else's. Lots of guys can run up points, but can they do it when the game is on the line? Can they perform at their best when the situation calls for composure under pressure? You don't really know until the situation arises and they come through in the clutch.

I would like to think that I scored my share of clutch goals, including that one to tie the score late in Game 6 of the 1987 Stanley Cup Final against the Edmonton Oilers. It was a do-or-die situation. It happened a long time ago, but I remember that my teammates and I weren't intimidated by the moment, even though we were playing a bunch of future Hall of Famers.

We went on to win that game and force a Game 7. Even though the Oilers won that ultimate test, the memory of doing the best we could under extreme circumstances remains clear in my mind.

Perhaps the most clutch player I ever had to compete with was Bob Clarke. He did everything well from a technical standpoint, but he also knew how to rise to the occasion. How about the overtime goal he scored in Game 2 of the 1974 Stanley Cup Final? This game was played at Boston, where the Flyers seemed to almost never win. Clarke fired a shot from the right circle and when the puck hit the net, he leaped in the air—half in joy, half in amazement that the curse had finally been lifted. It might have been the most clutch goal I've ever witnessed. A few days later, the Flyers won their first championship at the Spectrum, and who can forget that video of Clarke and Bernie Parent lugging Lord Stanley's silverware around the ice and Clarke giving that sly wink and a smile to the camera? That's probably one of the most iconic photographs in Flyers history.

Clarke was simply a great leader. There were times when he got cut, like a gash over his eye and blood dripping down his jersey, and he simply refused to go to the locker room for treatment. Just kept right on playing. It was an honor to play for him. You wanted to play well with him, in part, because you didn't dare not give your best and let him down.

Mark Howe was cut from the same fabric. The Flyers defenseman had that knack for playing his best hockey when all the chips were on the table. Maybe he got some of that from his old man, Gordie. His hockey talent was so evident that guys on the bench would watch what he was doing even when he didn't have the puck! His skating ability allowed him to take chances because if he turned the puck over, he would simply outrace wingers heading back into the Flyers' zone. One year he had seven short-handed goals—seven! That's more than some forwards get in a career. (By the way, those seven shorties tied a team record held by a forward named Propp.)

If you want the epitome of a clutch player, it would be Tim Kerr. In addition to holding the single-season record for power-play goals, he scored 50 or more goals in four straight seasons and a lot of them either tied or won games for the Flyers. There was that four-goal game in the playoffs. If that isn't clutch, what is?

I couldn't finish this list without including one of the most clutch competitors I have ever played with: Dave Poulin.

What Flyers fan of a certain age doesn't remember the playoff goal he scored in the 1985 Eastern Conference finals series with the old Quebec Nordiques at the Spectrum? It was a best-of-seven series, and this was Game 6, with the Flyers up three games to two.

With a trip to the Stanley Cup Final on the line, the Flyers were clinging to a 1–0 lead in the second period when they found themselves down two men with Quebec looking to tie.

That's when captain Dave Poulin found the puck on his stick with a full sheet of ice in front of him. On a breakaway, Poulin beat Mario Gosselin high to the glove side to give the Flyers a 2–0 lead. They would win the game 3–0, advancing to the final round against Edmonton.

That goal changed the momentum of the game and was one of the greatest solo plays in Flyers history. Does it get any more clutch than that?

When I headed to Boston in 1990, I had the pleasure of sharing the same ice with Ray Bourque. While he might not have been as shifty or quite as quick as Bobby Orr, he sure knew how to rise to the occasion when it mattered most. Ray did everything well. Like Howe, he anticipated what the other team was trying to do offensively. And if the other team turned the puck over, he could lead the counter-rush or dish it to a breaking teammate. I would put him right up there with some of the best to ever play that position.

During that same year when the Bruins made it to the Final, forward Cam Neely had a chance to show what he could do as the prototype power forward. He was so hard to knock off the puck. Great balance, and a knack for making something happen in heavy traffic. While he won plenty of games with goals, he was equally adept at getting back on defense.

After the season in Boston and the decision to sign with the North Stars, I had a chance to watch Minnesota center Mike Modano as he just got started in the NHL. He was a joy to follow. Very creative offensively with a penchant for scoring the big goal. He was just getting his feet wet in the top league, but he was a quick learner. If you skated as well as Modano or shot the puck the way he did, you were bound to score some clutch goals.

Another North Star, Neal Broten, was a crafty player who always found a way to win. He controlled the power play for Minnesota. He had a knack for hanging on to the puck and not giving it away, which is so crucial with the man advantage. A quiet guy but an excellent leader. After 15 years in the North Stars organization, he wound up with the New Jersey Devils for the 1994–95 season. So what happened? In the Cup-clinching game against Detroit, he scored what turned out to be the game-winner. How clutch does it get?

Then you had Chris Pronger. He and I crossed paths in Hartford, and he assisted on the goal that became my 1,000th NHL point. I had no idea he would go on to have the kind of career he enjoyed. Give my old pal Brad McCrimmon some of the credit for showing "Prongs" how to play the game the right way.

As for my All-Opponent Clutch team, the first selection might surprise you a bit, but I can vouch for how well he played in the big moments—Edmonton goaltender Grant Fuhr. While the Oilers' position players were getting a lot of the credit for those first couple Stanley Cups in the mid-'80s, it was Fuhr who saved some of his best work for when the time called for it. He might have been the toughest goaltender to score against I have ever faced, with lightning-quick reflexes and great anticipation on the shooting angles. When the action got hot and heavy, he didn't overreact or get caught out of position. And he played just as fresh in the third period as he did in the first.

Gee, there were nights when I must have had bad dreams about the Islanders' Bryan Trottier. Defensively, he could check you in the blink of an eye. And when Mike Bossy started drawing all the defensive attention away (Bossy had nine straight seasons of 50 goals or more), Trots cleaned up. Might I add that he was from my home province, Saskatchewan, and if you don't know how to play both ends of the rink, you'd better not acknowledge you're from there. Trottier certainly did. He was a big part of the Islanders' four straight Stanley Cups.

Then you had Montreal's Guy Lafleur, who made scoring look easy, just like Bossy did. He would race down the right wing with those long locks flowing and get the Montreal Forum faithful out of their seats with some impossible angle shot. "The Flower" could snipe with the best of them and always had a knack for getting the big goal when it mattered most. I got to play against him quite often and could never see a soft spot in his game. In the closing minutes of a close game, Guy wanted the puck on his stick, and he often did magical things with it.

Quebec's Peter Šťastný ranks right up there on my list of all-time clutch players. In my book, he was underrated because he played for the Nordiques and they didn't seem to get that much media attention, maybe because the Canadiens were so established in Canada folklore. We managed to beat the Nordiques in the 1985 playoffs but guys like Šťastný didn't make it easy. If he had played in New York, Boston, or Chicago, he probably would have been a more recognized player.

Brett Hull could shoot the puck just about as hard as his father, Bobby. Brett had a quick release and could score goals in bunches. Perhaps his most famous goal was the one that clinched the Cup for the Dallas Stars in 1999. Some say his foot was in the crease on the overtime goal, others say it wasn't. Anyway, it's all history now. The thing a lot of people don't know is that later in his career he became a much better defensive, complete player. I know I didn't look forward to playing against him.

Right up there for toughness to play against was goaltender Patrick Roy, who stood out for many years in Montreal but also starred in Denver. There wasn't a shot he couldn't stop. People thought he was finished when he talked his way out of Montreal, but he resurrected his career in Denver and has to be considered one of the best to ever play the position.

Finally, what more can be said about Jaromír Jágr? In terms of points, he's second only to Gretzky. One-on-one, his strength almost overpowered you. How many yards of video show him using that balance and muscle to blast around NHL defensemen? Sure, he was gifted but he also worked quite hard, which is why he lasted in the NHL up to his forties.

Now if you're looking for the best clutch player in today's game, I would have to say it's Sidney Crosby, who has won the Stanley Cup three times with the Pittsburgh Penguins. Everyone thinks of Crosby as just a scoring machine, but he's also very conscientious about his defensive play. In my eyes, he's one of the best to ever play the game because he will do whatever it takes to win.

I also like what I see of Colorado's Nathan MacKinnon and Edmonton's Connor McDavid. Both guys have the speed to cover both ends of the rink. I expect them to play the game at a high level for years to come.

Right up there with Sid is Russian superstar Alexander Ovechkin, who had his sights set on breaking Gretzky's goals record. The guy is as strong as an ox and loves to score the big goal late in games to decide the outcome. His shot is so fast and so powerful, I have to chuckle. No way I'm getting in front of that thing.

CHAPTER 9

THE LINDBERGH TRAGEDY

SWEDISH GOALTENDER PELLE LINDBERGH and I were drafted by the Flyers the same year, 1979. Even though we came from vastly different cultures, we eventually formed a close bond. While I was scoring goals during an NHL-record streak of 35 straight games without a loss and helping Philadelphia reach the 1980 Stanley Cup Final, Pelle was busy playing goaltender for Sweden at the Lake Placid Winter Olympics and became the only goaltender to take a point (a 2–2 tie) off the eventual gold medal USA team.

The summer after Lindbergh helped Sweden win the bronze medal in upstate New York, he reported to the Flyers' Maine Mariners minor league team in Portland. For the first couple years I really didn't get to know him because he was playing for the farm team. But after two seasons in Maine, he was ready to make the jump to the NHL and that's when I got to know him much better. We shared one thing in common: we loved to compete. I loved to score on him in practice. I knew his weaknesses, although there weren't many. Putting the puck in against him was even more fun than when I scored on the volatile Ron Hextall in later years.

I don't know if it was the language barrier, but Pelle didn't say much. But his smile was always present, and it was special for me because later, after he was gone, I thought about that a lot and realized how special it was. He always made practice a little more memorable.

In the 1984–85 season Pelle won the Vezina Trophy as the NHL's best goaltender, and that was really extraordinary for a lot of us. He was just coming into his own and it seemed like the sky was the limit as one of the best goaltenders in the National Hockey League. He was one of the big reasons why we were able to make it to the Stanley Cup Final at the end of that season against the high-powered Edmonton Oilers.

We were a little (or perhaps a lot) overmatched in that five-game setback to Gretzky & Co. But going into the 1985–86 season, the future looked very bright. We had one of the best young goaltenders in pro hockey, and anyone can tell you that's probably the most crucial position in ice hockey.

All that optimism changed early on the morning of November 10, 1985. The previous night the Flyers had defeated Boston by a 5–3 score. Even though Lindbergh didn't play in that game, he sort of waived his light drinking policy in favor of some serious imbibing. Pelle owned a high-powered Porsche automobile, and this was a formula for trouble. After leaving a local nightclub in Voorhees with two friends, Lindbergh proceeded to climb into the model 930 Turbo, reach a high speed, and crash it into a wall at the juncture of Somerdale Road and Ogg Avenue in Somerdale, New Jersey. Lindbergh, 26, wound up clinically brain-dead, and his two passengers were seriously injured in the crash.

Some of the timing of the crash might have had to do with the fact the Flyers were off the next two days, and Pelle planned to attend a boat show in Atlantic City the next day.

We all knew Pelle was drinking a lot that night. I was actually taking a couple days off from the alcohol because I was seriously into fixing up my house down at the shore. When I heard that he was in the crash, I immediately went to the hospital. I was able to see him at the end. It was really a bad situation. His fiancée, Kerstin Pietzsch, and his mom, Anna-Lisa, had been staying with him. It was just a tragic thing. The doctors were able to keep him on life support until his father, the late Sigge Lindbergh, could fly in from Sweden.

The news shocked everyone in the hockey community and all the Flyers fans. A lot of people knew Pelle was not a serious drinker, which made the whole story sound rather bizarre. Whenever I was around, he had Coca-Colas all the time. Later I went back to see the spot where he had crashed. There were just little concrete stairs there. Otherwise, the car might have passed over that piece of ground and possibly caused less damage.

Hockey fans around the world were in disbelief. Pelle had won the American Hockey League's MVP and Rookie of the Year awards in 1981. Then, just a couple seasons later, he was playing in the NHL All-Star Game and was named to the NHL All-Rookie team. Later, he became the first European goaltender to win the coveted Vezina Trophy.

No one was more shocked than his teammates. It was hard to imagine a team going on and doing its best without one of its best players at a key position.

After all, this was a young man who knew his limitations when it came to nightlife. It just didn't fit his personality. He really wasn't into loud storytelling or listening to others boast of their accomplishments. On the road, he did tag along with others, but he gave the distinct impression he wanted to follow rules, such as curfew.

Guys on the team respected that. While there might have been a "frat boy" mentality at certain times in certain situations, no one was pressured into doing something they didn't want to do, at least as far as veterans were concerned. There might have been some rookie hazing at times, but Pelle was well past that.

At that point, all thoughts and prayers went out to Pelle the person as opposed to Pelle the goaltender. But you couldn't help but wonder what the next 10 years would have been like if his career had been allowed to continue. Maybe a Vezina Trophy here or there. He had already won one. Or perhaps even a Stanley Cup or two. We knew from being in the championship round against Edmonton the year before that he had the right stuff. He was intimidated by some of the best hockey players in the world.

Eventually the entire team showed up at the hospital and stood around waiting to get word of Pelle's condition. Fortunately, we had good leadership that year with captain Dave Poulin and veterans such as Mark Howe and Brad McCrimmon. We got together at coach Mike Keenan's house every day until the next game, which was Thursday, November 14. We got together because we wanted to stick together as a team. It helped to vocalize some of your feelings. The team's sports psychologist, Steve Rosenberg, helped us all, too. He had a chance to talk to everybody and discuss what they were thinking about. The way I recall it, these sessions were somewhat therapeutic.

In that year we had four rookies (Rick Tocchet, Scott Mellanby, Peter Zezel, and Derrick Smith). They were fairly new to the pro game and certainly to this kind of tragedy. The Flyers were a close-knit bunch, be they young or old, and that's how we managed to get through everything. That season started off so promising. Whenever Pelle was in goal, we figured we were going to win. In fact, in the eight games he played in that season, he had a record of 6–2–0 with a goals-against average under 3.

It was to the point where we were thinking to ourselves, *With this guy in goal we might just win a couple Stanley Cups.* It's just too bad and led to a lot of speculation about what our chances of winning it all would have been if the accident had not happened.

The impact of Lindbergh's death went far beyond what it meant to the team on the ice. He was an immensely popular player—among his teammates, the fans, and the hockey world as a whole. Fun-loving, free-spirited, kind, generous, and laid-back, Lindbergh had a special gift for making friends and drawing a crowd wherever he went. Moreover, he had planned to get married in the 1986 offseason. In the blink of an eye, he was gone.

I can't imagine what the reaction was like back in his native Sweden. I suspect he was considered a national hero, going back to his days in the 1980 Winter Olympics. Like Canadians, Swedes are known for their love of hockey, and this loss had to hit everyone pretty hard.

It's been nearly 40 years since his passing, but I still think about him all the time and what might have been. He was a special person, and those types of people don't come along that often.

CHAPTER 10

UNSPORTSMANLIKE CONDUCT

J UST ABOUT EVERYONE in their youth has run across a school-yard bully—usually a kid who gets his kicks by physically intimidating those who have no interest in confrontation. Some of these aggressive types outgrow that sort of behavior; others don't.

One who apparently didn't was former NHL defenseman Chris Chelios, a blueliner who decided his pure hockey skill wasn't enough. He played 26 seasons in the league, and let the record show that on numerous occasions he crossed the line and deliberately tried to injure players.

I was one of them.

The Flyers were performing beyond expectations in the 1989 Stanley Cup playoffs. They made it all the way to the Eastern Conference Finals against the Montreal Canadiens. One of the backliners on that team was Chelios, and while we didn't exactly have a friendly rivalry in the five or six seasons leading up to this series, I was totally unprepared for what happened in the very first game at the old Montreal Forum.

Let me set the stage about the kind of person Chelios is. He owned a couple restaurants, and he had a couple workers at these establishments who were stabbed to death in 2007. In 2009, he had a driving under the influence incident in Chicago. His truck had to be towed away from the scene of the indiscretion.

The thing about Chelios is he loved picking on the skilled players—whether it was cheap shots or cross-checks or slashes—but he hated going up against the tougher players. He wouldn't fight them, but he went out of his way to pick on the skill players. I always liked tough guy Dale Hunter because he had an extreme dislike for Chelios. Hunter would hit Chelios whenever he could, so there were the usual crocodile tears and pleading his case to the referees.

I don't respect Chelios. He might be in the Hockey Hall of Fame, but I guess the voters for his induction overlooked a lot or just weren't paying attention.

One incident must have clearly escaped their attention— Game 1 of that '89 series at the Forum. The Flyers had just finished a Game 7 elimination of the Pittsburgh Penguins. That wasn't really very easy because Mario Lemieux and the Penguins were just a couple years away from their first two-year run with the Stanley Cup.

I was leading the entire playoffs in scoring when we arrived at the Forum on May 1. As I was skating along the boards, Chelios skated up and hit me from behind, elbowing me in the head with a dirty shot that sent me crashing into the unforgiving metal stanchion that holds the panels of glass in place.

I could have died from that hit. And I almost did. I may have been unconscious before my prone body was fully extended after hitting the ice. Incredibly, there was no penalty on the play. Chelios should have received a 20-game suspension for that egregious act. He didn't even receive a fine. Head trainer Pat Croce and team doctor Gary Dorshimer were there, and they were concerned because I was in and out of consciousness the entire day. I had to remain in the hospital all night, and hospital staff had to keep getting me out of bed and walking with me in the hallways because they weren't sure of my condition, and didn't want me to fall into a deep sleep.

I don't have too much in the way of memories from those first 24 hours after the near-death experience. I do know that my family members were deeply concerned about my welfare and did their best to send best wishes for a speedy recovery.

As the hours went by, I was still feeling a lot of uncertainty about my overall state of mind. Given the circumstances and knowing my team needed me, I wanted to get back as soon as possible. On the other side of the coin, getting back on the ice again after a hit like that kind of lowered my confidence level to perform at the highest level. It's hard to be at your best if you're constantly looking over your shoulder.

The troubled looks on the faces of Croce and Dorshimer told me they might have also had some doubts about me returning to action so quickly. Plus, the coaching staff had to be wondering about my overall state of mind. What happened if I got hammered again and suffered some lingering damage? It was something everyone in the organization had to be thinking about.

The thing that really bothered me is that Chelios was never sorry that he did it. He always bragged about how he's a good player and he didn't do anything. But the Flyers, and me in particular, knew better than that. Thankfully, I missed just one game. With the concussion, I had to pass all the baseline tests before I could play again. But I was able to play in Games 3, 4, 5, and 6. I did play well in those games, but after that hit, things were never really quite the same. I was really nervous, because I didn't want to get hit that hard again.

It took me a couple years for me to fully recover from a mental standpoint. Years went by before I was able to play without thinking about what had happened in Montreal with Chelios.

Whenever I got hit during those ensuing years, it was still in the back of my mind. Was this happening again? Was this another dirty check? And would it cause a "relapse?" It was hard not to think about.

Then, thankfully, our goalie, Ron Hextall, went after Chelios to exact some revenge late in Game 6. With approximately two minutes to go, down 4–2, the Flyers were about to lose and be eliminated when Hextall went off, connecting with a few pretty good punches well away from his crease. For his heroics, "Hexy" earned a 12-game suspension, to be served at the start of the 1989–90 campaign.

Even Chelios admired Hextall for sticking up for a teammate. He said that if he had been a goalie and something like that had happened to one of his teammates, he probably would have done exactly what Hextall did.

I felt the same way. Hextall backed me up. I love him for that and the leadership he displayed in doing that. The skirmish was almost comical. Hextall was throwing punches with both hands in windmill fashion and even heaved his blocker glove at the guy. I thought the dozen games' banishment Hextall received was brutal. To this day, I still admire him for doing that.

After a quick trade to Boston during the 1989–90 season, it was off to Minnesota courtesy of a trade engineered by my old teammate and mentor, Bob Clarke, who was now general manager of the North Stars. But wouldn't you know it, now I was in the Central Division and playing on a regular basis against the Chicago Blackhawks, who had just traded for some guy named Chelios. As fate would have it, we wound up playing the Windy City crew in the first round of the 1991 playoffs and beat them. Of course, I should mention that a key to the series was the Blackhawks' penchant for taking bad penalties. Chelios took a lot of the blame for that.

The North Stars had a great power play that year. I remember the first game in Chicago went to overtime. I scored the game-winner, and the feeling couldn't have been sweeter. That goal really sent us on our way and eventually we made the Final that year. In that series against Chicago, Chelios was up to his usual cheap-shot tactics. Out of the blue he just punched me in the head when I wasn't looking. As I mentioned, he never fought the tough guys. But that's the way he was—just punched me right in the head.

The hard feelings extended off the ice. In 2011, I was at Brad McCrimmon's funeral after he was killed in the plane crash in Russia. Chelios had a chance to say something to me, but he didn't. He wasn't sorry about anything.

Recently, on a Facebook post to a Flyers fan, Chelios boasted that he "decapitated Propp" and beat up Hextall in the grudge match. That wasn't a very cordial thing to say. I really don't know why he would say that, because I never did anything to him. But that's just the way he is. I don't think of him as a good person. Maybe he was popular among players because he drank a lot, partied a lot. It was tough for me because after that series in '89, it took a while to recover. You can lose your career due to something like that. But I will always be thankful that I was able to recover. Having said that, I will never forget that hit from behind.

Most of the fans in Philadelphia still hate him because of that hit. They think of him as a dirty player, and so do I. I've talked to a lot of other people, and they say the same thing. I haven't responded in the past, but here is a chance to state that I think he's an ass.

Chelios is not like me. I never went out of my way to hurt somebody or hate somebody. But I will make an exception for Chelios, because I hate what he did. Recently, he was let go by ESPN. He's a nasty guy. Maybe he deserved what he got.

In almost any professional sports team's locker room, there is a small faction of players—maybe as few as one—who just aren't happy with their situation and can get vocal about it. It can be something as trivial as not getting one's skates sharpened to their liking all the way up to how much money they're making.

Generally topping the list: the coach.

Some players will keep it to themselves if they don't like the way they are being used or the amount of playing time they are getting. Or, in some instances, they will lean over to the guy sitting a locker away and whine about something.

If a team isn't performing well, the locker room provides a fertile atmosphere for this sort of complaining. Ultimately, if things get too out of hand, it can bring a team down.

Such was the case with the Flyers during the 1987–88 season. This was during coach Mike Keenan's last go-round in Philadelphia. Under Keenan, the Flyers had made it to the Stanley Cup Final twice, including a Game 7 series in 1987, which could have gone either way.

By now we know that it wasn't easy playing for this demanding coach. While with the Flyers, Keenan never seemed to let a player get comfortable with him. There was always a lot of uncertainty—mind games, if you will. This mindset worked, and worked well, for a few years but the expiration date arrived rather abruptly.

Keenan was hard on his players. I remember we had a meeting in 1988 when we talked about everybody on the team. The discussion was about whether we wanted to get him fired. Ultimately it was decided that such a move wouldn't be perceived well among the public, so the decision was made to keep him. But a lot of people didn't like the way he coached after four years. Eventually, in May, Flyers general manager Bob Clarke fired Keenan after a 38–33–9 record and a first-round playoff exit.

Clarke felt Keenan was destroying the confidence of the young players with his quick hooks and harsh language. Keenan felt

Clarke undermined him by lending a sympathetic ear to players' complaints. Keenan once told Scott Mellanby the only reason he was on the roster was because he was a Clarke favorite. The coach also once told Ron Sutter if he didn't try harder, he was going to bench his twin brother, Rich.

I watched with morbid curiosity as all this was going on. I'm always willing to give a coach the benefit of the doubt so as long as we were winning, I didn't pay it too much attention.

So the meetings continued, although I wasn't crazy about them. In fact, I always supported Keenan because I was a good player and I lobbied to keep him as the coach. Meanwhile, the Flyers were aware that some new, younger players were making their way up the pipeline and to make room for them, some veterans had to go. That's why Poulin, Kerr, and I had to pack up our gear and move to different teams. It wasn't easy for any of us but, in general, we knew it was time to go. We saw the writing on the wall.

Oddly enough, the younger players coming in didn't necessarily have what it takes to win in the NHL, as evidenced by five straight seasons out of the playoffs. Losing leaders like the three of us no doubt hurt their chances of making the postseason.

I always thought there was a lot going on with internal politics on the Flyers, but when I got to the North Stars it was more of the same. Coach Bob Gainey had his mind made up on certain players (don't they all?). He preferred playing veteran players who were accustomed to how the left-wing lock style of defense worked. The guys who could play this system weren't really great scorers, so the Stars had to rely on their defensive players to keep the scores down.

Believe me, there was quite a lot of mumbling about that. No one wants to spend the whole night trying to chase some of the top opposing players all night long. As a result of the whining, a couple people got traded. I heard some of this mumbling and wondered if subconsciously it was hurting the team's performance.

When I arrived in Hartford, Paul Holmgren was the coach. Then he moved to GM and Pierre McGuire came in to coach. There were lots of injuries. Now I had been reduced to an injury fill-in. That's why I played as many games as I did. Believe it or not, I got a bonus for every game I played.

Suffice it to say, I just worked hard and kept my mouth shut. Even though we had good defensemen like Brad McCrimmon and Chris Pronger, there were guys who would openly complain about the state of the team or how it was being run. All the instability at coach and the front office made it difficult for everybody at that time.

After much thought, I decided to retire. Things weren't going to get any better any time soon. Injuries were keeping me from performing as well as I could.

A lot of teams, when they hit close to rock bottom and don't have a lot of star players, find they have a lot of well-paid complainers. It's as if everyone's at fault except the complainers themselves. In my opinion, if they played harder for their coach and complained a little less, everyone would be better off, and a franchise comeback would happen a lot sooner.

Now, there's so much money to be made, there's probably no reason to complain. Coaches are hired to get fired. There are a lot of players who make "set-for-life" money. They only need to play four or five years, which is about the average length of a career now. They just take advantage of the situation and then they're out the door.

CHAPTER 11

THE BRAWL IN MONTREAL

SOME HOCKEY FIGHTS can make you want to grab the armrests on your chair. If they get really intense, they can get you to jump to your feet.

Or, if you happened to be witness to the infamous "Brawl in Montreal" on May 14, 1987, you might even smile, chuckle, and high-five the guy one seat over. Regular hockey fights are a dime a dozen, but this one looked like a scene right out of the theater of the absurd. Players scurrying onto the ice from their locker rooms half-dressed or lacking the proper footwear. Pregame fans pointing at the ever-growing crowd on the Montreal Forum's famous playing surface. Even veteran fans of the hockey battles standing with mouths slightly agape.

It was supposed to be your average pregame warm-up session—when players take part in light skating and shooting drills to get the kinks out. A lot of people usually head to the refreshment stands or restrooms to get ready for the real thing. On this particular night, the minutes leading up to the game were most certainly an unreal thing.

This was Game 6 of the Prince of Wales Conference Final. Holding a 3–2 lead in the best-of-seven series, the Flyers were in position to, with a win, move on to their second Stanley Cup

Final in three years. Emotions were high and things were getting testy even as the two teams skated around prior to the game. The Flyers decided to dress some extra players—even though most, if not all, of them were not going to play in the game—in case someone couldn't play. We had about 24 players in the warm-ups, but only 20 can actually play in the game.

That's probably why someone like our defenseman Ed Hospodar might have had a bit of a devil-may-care attitude. It certainly was a recipe for mayhem, because the Habs had this tradition of ending a warm-up by firing a puck down the ice into an opponent's vacant net. Well, there were only two Flyers—Hospodar and backup goaltender Glenn "Chico" Resch—still on the ice. As a team, we knew the Canadiens might try to do this at our expense. Montreal also had two players still skating around: bad boy Claude Lemieux and tough guy Shayne Corson. Hospodar told Lemieux not to even make an attempt at the goal, and for a moment Lemieux appeared to listen.

It looked like controversy might be avoided when all four players left the ice. But Lemieux and Corson managed to sneak back onto the ice, and that's when all hell broke loose. And it changed the game of hockey forever. Hospodar and Resch raced back onto the ice when they saw Lemieux and Corson there. Soon players from both teams poured out of the dressing rooms. Dave Brown, minus most of his game equipment, was one of the first Flyers to reach the ice. He immediately got into it with Montreal bruiser Chris Nilan. They must have been locked together for a good five minutes.

While all this was going on, there were no referees or linesmen to be found. They were back in their changing room getting ready for the game. What this meant was there was no one to break up any of the skirmishes, and my guess is there were too many fights going on for four men to do much to stop most of them. It was really getting out of control. One of our tough guys, Don Nachbaur, took a swing at Hall of Famer Larry Robinson and connected. That can be found on a highlight (or lowlight) film somewhere.

A bench-clearing (or in this case, locker-room-clearing) brawl might have been bonus entertainment for some people back then, but it really had very little to do with the sport of hockey. The game is supposed to be about speed, dexterity, and flashbulb moments when someone scores an amazing goal or a goalie comes up with a fabulous save.

This incident, coming as it did in the Stanley Cup playoffs, did very little to enhance hockey's image in many people's eyes. Very likely a vast number of people were turned off by all this contrived sideshow violence and some possibly disengaged from the sport. Competition for the Stanley Cup pits the best against the best, and if a sideshow like the one in Montreal is allowed to go on, it just detracts from the final product. The NHL has always tried to attract new friends, not alienate its loyal followers. The outcry in the media certainly didn't help the cause much when it came to the casual fan who might be on the fence about buying tickets.

If the whole idea of this brawl was to somehow intimidate the opponent, it came up short. The days of the "Broad Street Bullies" were coming to an end.

The whole thing must have lasted at least 20 minutes. I still have images of guys like our defenseman Doug Crossman jumping onto the ice with just his flip-flops on and trying to make his way to the big scrum. It was rather crazy and somewhat comical. As soon as one fight was brought under control, another one started. If there was any question about bad blood between the two teams, it was answered right there and then. It was crazy but exciting at the same time. Finally, the on-ice officials showed up and attempted to restore some order. Not all the Flyers took part in this brouhaha. Our coach, Mike Keenan, made sure our starting goaltender Ron Hextall did not join in the proceedings, even though "Hexy" was itching to get out there. Keenan didn't want Hextall getting injured or suspended.

This all took place a little more than a decade after the Flyers had won their two Stanley Cups in 1974 and 1975. During that championship run, the infamous Bullies had ridden roughshod over the NHL and the league clearly was exasperated by those tactics. Without a doubt it saw a chance to compose a mandate against fighting. Even in the '80s, we had tough teams. Brown was the toughest. Daryl Stanley could go with the best of them. Rick Tocchet had 288 penalty minutes that season; need I say more? Hospodar didn't need much to drop the gloves.

It's safe to say that donnybrook was pretty much the last of its kind. Hospodar was banned for the rest of the playoffs; a lot of others got fined. This square-off came just a couple months after a nasty fracas between Boston and Quebec, and the battles were becoming more commonplace. Later that summer, the NHL instituted Rule 70.1 to penalize players who left the bench to engage in a fight (an automatic 10-game suspension and $10,000 fine, which was a lot of money at the time). Ditto coaches who lost control of their players. Someone told me Los Angeles Kings defenseman Randy Holt got fired up and once skated over to the Flyers bench and said, "What are you going to do about it?" And about six Flyers jumped over the boards to answer the call.

Those days have been over for a long time.

———————

Long ago, some predicted hockey would evolve past fighting and become more of a gentleman's sport.

How did that go?

While the total number of penalty minutes for exchanging punches may have gone down in recent years, there's still the age-old tradition of sticking up for a wrong, such as the bullying of a teammate or a random cheap shot. Don't tell me you've ever been to a hockey game where a fight broke out, the whole place stood up, and you just sat there disinterested. No, you jumped up like everybody else to see how this manly conflict was going to end.

Let's remember, I jumped into pro hockey just as the heyday of the Broad Street Bullies was winding down. By 1979, several of the Flyers' chief protagonists, such as Dave Schultz, Don Saleski, and Ed Van Impe, had changed addresses. But André "Moose" Dupont was still on the roster, and some new blood like Mel Bridgman and Behn Wilson were the up-and-coming sheriffs in town.

In my book, pound for pound and punch for punch, Wilson was about as dangerous as they come. His reputation grew leaps and bounds after he scored a one-punch knockout of a guy in Detroit and only grew from there. Wilson earned the ultimate praise a fighter could receive: "He's crazy!" Well, you had to be a little nuts to take on a behemoth like the Islanders' Clark Gillies, who packed a mean punch of his own. More than once, the two men stood toe-to-toe and there wasn't a single fanny sitting on a seat when those two went at it either at the old Spectrum or the Nassau Coliseum.

I got to know Wilson, and he was crazy in sort of a fun way. His strength was unquestioned. Most of the time he was simply this mild, quiet guy, but when he got into a fight, he just lost all semblance of composure. Even the guys on the bench appreciated these tussles. Early on we learned to bang our sticks on the boards as soon as the fight was over and, believe me, there was a lot of stick-banging and grinning whenever "Big Behn" dropped the gloves.

Bridgman was cast from the same mold. He wore that droopy mustache and seemed to have a perpetual scowl. Believe it or not, he was a No. 1 overall draft pick (the only one the Flyers have ever had), and he cut his teeth by taking on Boston tough guy Terry O'Reilly, who had come up with the Big, Bad Bruins. These two went at it several times in front of grinning, hollering fans at the old Boston Garden. Again, a lot rode on these skirmishes. If one guy scored a decisive victory—which seldom happened—then momentum might shift to the winner's team. Mel fought O'Reilly and he didn't back down. I had first-row seats on the Flyers' bench for those exchanges, and they stand out in my memory.

In other professional sports, big, bad fights break out once or twice a year. In hockey, it's more like once or twice a night. Why so frequently? Do players go at it just to uphold their honor or that of the team? Well, having witnessed enough tussles this side of Al Bernstein, there are plenty of motives.

For instance, if a team falls behind 2–0 and its players look like they were out rather late the night before, then a good old-fashioned square-off instigated by a player from the trailing squad can change the negative mojo, especially in front of a home crowd. If it's a powerhouse exchange between two heavyweights, then players on the bench will be banging their sticks on the boards and wearing appreciative grins when the skirmish is over.

Also, a big, borderline hit on a smaller teammate can cause an enforcer to challenge one of the offending team's tough personalities. "Don't mess with one of my guys!" seems to be the message. It's a time-honored tradition.

Sometimes people's reputations proceed them. Nobody in the '50s and '60s wanted anything to do with Gordie Howe. Later, even the most proficient fighters tended to steer clear of Gillies. But remember—hardly anybody goes undefeated. That's the hook that keeps 'em standing in the aisles at hockey games.

I should mention the infamous fight between my former teammate and later coach, Paul Holmgren, and Boston's Wayne Cashman during and after a preseason game in 1977 at the Spectrum. I wasn't there yet but I've heard the story a million times. Both guys got ejected and headed for the locker room, but when they saw each other in the hallway, they went at it again. To prevent a recurrence, Flyers officials installed a steel gate between locker rooms. That was still in place when the Spectrum closed in 2009. Now I'm told it sits in storage at the Wells Fargo Center.

Homer could go with the best of them. Like Wilson, he would always size up an opponent with that icy stare. Paul didn't win every fight, but he seldom lost by a decisive margin.

Now, right up there with Wilson, Bridgman, and Holmgren was a 6'4", 225-pound lefty by the name of Dave Brown. Some people have him as the Flyers' top fighter of all time because he had an iron jaw, and some guys didn't know how to handle someone who threw punches with his left hand. More than one guy hit the ice after a Brown haymaker simply because he wasn't prepared for the angle of the punch. Dave was a great fighter. Perhaps his best work was done in that playoff game at Montreal in 1987. He wasn't wearing a jersey so there was nothing holding him back. Dave went at it with Nilan, and that's one for the video record books. On and off, they went at it for what seemed like 10 minutes. It was a classic. I don't know how they played a game after that one.

Another tough guy on my side of the puck was Glen Cochrane. Outwardly, he acted as crazy as a bedbug. He had this maneuver where he would try to get out of his jersey as quickly as possible—not only for more arm freedom, but also to prevent the other guy from having something to grab onto. He had this fight with one of the New Jersey Devils named Hector Marini. That one ended pretty quickly and served notice that Glen would be a force to be reckoned with.

As nasty as he was, Glen had a sweet side. Not many people know this, but when his sister needed a bone marrow transplant, Glen was on the phone in two seconds. These two were a match, and that's a rare thing, so what Glen did was both generous and noteworthy.

Not much has to be said about Tocchet. He had this jackhammer style of throwing punches with his right hand. This was on display in the famous 1987 match with the Leafs' Wendel Clark at the old Maple Leaf Gardens. The guys on the bench were riveted to this fight. The two stood toe-to-toe for a good 50 seconds with almost no defense. Just back-and-forth bombs, neither man giving an inch. The thing about Tocchet was he was a great all-around player, not just a goon. He posted 48 goals one season and, after a trade, was a big part of Pittsburgh's 1992 Stanley Cup championship team.

Now here's a surprise for you—Tim Kerr put together four straight 50-goal-plus seasons, but he was also an underestimated fighter. He had the size (6'4") and the balance. Like Brown, he was a lefty and caught a lot of guys off-guard coming with punches from the non-traditional side. The guy was as strong as they come, which is partly why he was so hard to knock off-balance in the slot. Tim didn't fight much but when someone acted out, he was ready to go.

At the end of the 1989–90 season, when I was in Boston, I met Lyndon Byers. Like me, he was from Saskatchewan, so naturally we hit it off. Lyndon did his job in an efficient way. We roomed together for about a month at the end of the regular season plus the playoffs. We talked about his role all the time.

When I got to Minnesota in 1991, I grew to appreciate the fighting skills of one Basil McRae. He was a tough guy. Ever competitive, he could give someone a bloody nose in a hurry, and he was an exceptional enforcer for the North Stars. When I first got there and arrived in training camp, I beat him in the sit-up contest, and he hated to lose to me because he was so competitive. We had a good laugh over that one.

CHAPTER 12

McCRIMMON: A NATURAL-BORN LEADER

I N AN ENTIRE LIFETIME, a person might be fortunate enough to meet one or two people who not only become a friend but a role model as well. Often, it's someone who leads by example, a person who doesn't have to say much but forges a path simply by his actions.

Brad McCrimmon was just such a man.

I knew Brad was going to be a winner—and it turned out later he was, in 1989 when he led the Calgary Flames to their only Stanley Cup, defeating the Montreal Canadiens and my nemesis, Chris Chelios.

McCrimmon just had a way about him that seemed to rub off on other players. It's almost as if he expected to win every game he played in. He was a quick thinker and an outstanding player when it came to positioning himself on defense. Very seldom was he in the wrong place at the wrong time. He was a player from whom the other guys took their emotional cue, and he was seldom down. It was almost like having another coach on the bench—and this when he was barely out of his teens.

Here's a statistic to tell you the kind of savvy player he was: Brad finished with a career plus/minus rating of plus-448. That's the 10th best in National Hockey League history.

If anyone was paying attention back in the Brandon Wheat Kings days, they could almost have predicted something like that.

We both grew up in the province of Saskatchewan. Brad and his brother, Kelly, lived and worked on the family farm. Their parents, Byron and Faye, raised their boys the right way with an emphasis on strong, challenging work. I met Brad in the town of Prince Albert, whose hockey team, the Raiders, competed in the Saskatchewan Junior Hockey League. To put it bluntly, he was the best defenseman in the entire league at age 15 that year and I won Rookie of the Year, the scoring title, and the Most Valuable Player award at the same age while playing for the Melville Millionaires.

Oh, and did I mention we absolutely hated each other?

That's what made my 50th goal of the season extra sweet that season. We were playing at Prince Albert, and I was about to make an entry play when the fun started. The puck entered the zone. Brad went to pick it up, and he missed it. I grabbed the puck, went around him, and scored my milestone goal, all in front of the Prince Albert hometown fans. Needless to say, it looked like there was some steam coming out of the ears of the Raiders' coach and players. But we got a kick out of it.

I'll never forget that, and having the chance to do it at Brad's expense made it only that much more special. For years, I kept reminding him, and to his credit, he always took it the right way.

There were farmers in Dodsland who farmed grain, barley, and cattle. It was a no-nonsense environment, and maybe that's why Brad and I eventually began to hit it off when we found ourselves together on the Brandon Wheat Kings of the Western Hockey League the following year. Soon we were best friends. As the days and weeks passed, I realized what a great leader he was. Others looked up to him. We both loved talking about hockey with other players and going over strategy play by play.

The Brandon years were a lot of fun. McCrimmon always had a car, and since I didn't have one, I was hitching rides with him all the time. We had house parties on a regular basis because we weren't old enough to get into bars and other types of drinking establishments just yet. Still, there was lots of beer to be secured by somewhat nefarious means.

Recruiting enough people for these parties was hardly a problem. Brad was quite the ladies' man—he dated a lot and so he had plenty of guys at the parties after games. As we got older, the festivities moved into the bars, as we were now of legal age to drink. But to be clear, we didn't hang out in these joints on a regular basis because Brandon is a small town and word travels fast.

Brad's family did have a lake house nearby, and that was a fun place to hang out. We played golf when the weather was nice or played catch with a baseball. One of the highlights was a pig roast every weekend, followed up by a casual cigar. At these kinds of events, you can really bond with people.

Brad's and my lasting friendship really evolved in the three years we played together for the Wheat Kings. Future Flyer Ray Allison, a talented two-way forward, was also on that team. Brad quickly became one of the best defensemen in the league. One of the reasons he was so good was because he always had a smile on his face, plus his leadership skills were just incredible. He was mature way beyond his years, but he loved to have fun. Whether it was hockey or just about any subject, he was a great conversationalist. I was really quiet, and he was the exact opposite—and you know what they say about opposites.

Brad would frequently engage in conversation with coach Dunc McCallum. They would exchange ideas, especially during the times when we might need a bit of a change of strategies. That helped with the preparation to make us all better future pros. He wasn't the biggest defenseman at 5'11", 193 pounds, but if he was intent on hitting you, you knew about it. His smart, physical play helped land him on the 1978 Canada team at the World Junior Championships, and from what I've been told, he had a big hand in Canada's bronze medal that year.

McCallum was definitely a player-friendly coach. He always gave the team two cases of beer to share among ourselves during a long bus trip. These weren't your generic two- or three-hour journeys; more like six or seven hours. We certainly used that beer to "hydrate" ourselves.

This was back in the '70s, when you could still get away with this type of behavior. Today is a whole lot different. You won't find any beer on a junior hockey bus.

Our team kept getting better during Brad's and my three-year tenure together. By the third year, we made it to the Memorial Cup Final, which is the championship of Canadian junior hockey. I'm here to tell you that McCrimmon kid played nearly the entire game. He would play a complete shift, go to the bench, and at the very next whistle he would go out there again. Sometimes he didn't even come off. He was that good of a player. He didn't get winded.

Brad was acknowledged as a physical peacekeeper. He was often considered gruff and had a direct way of speaking that cultivated respect amongst his peers. He made our whole team better. Even though we eventually lost the championship game in overtime, we were proud with how far we had come and what we had accomplished.

At the end of our run in the WHL, it was time to move on to the NHL. Both of us were selected in the first round of the 1979 NHL Entry Draft. I went to the Flyers with the 14th pick in the first round, and Brad was taken by the Boston Bruins with the very next pick. That was another teasing point.

Little did we know we would be teammates just a few years later. In 1982, the Flyers decided they needed help on the back line, so they sent highly regarded goaltender Pete Peeters to the Bruins in a one-for-one trade to get McCrimmon. It's like we were destined to be together going back to the days before we even shaved.

Brad's rough-and-tumble style immediately fit into the Flyers' kind of play. They already had Brad Marsh, Glen Cochrane, Behn Wilson, and Frank Bathe. Besides, Flyers coach Bob McCammon argued that McCrimmon had been playing a little too much in the shadow of perennial All-Star Ray Bourque. It was a real kick to play with Brad in the National Hockey League. By then he was a best friend and someone I could trust, both on and off the ice.

Then things got even better for Brad and everyone on the Flyers when Philadelphia traded Ken Linseman and some draft picks to Hartford for Mark Howe, son of hockey immortal Gordie Howe. The Flyers' coaching staff was bright enough to pair them together, and there was instant chemistry between these two stars.

By our 1984–85 season, Mark and Brad were our two best defensemen. As a matter of fact, they were the top plus/minus pairing in the NHL for the decade of the 1980s. When the NHL began to give out an award for best plus/minus numbers in 1982–83, it was only a matter of time until either Howe or McCrimmon won it. In 1985–86, Howe did just that, taking the Emery Edge Award with a plus-87. McCrimmon finished second with plus-86. To top it off, Mark edged out Brad for the Barry Ashbee Trophy as the Flyers' top defenseman, though Brad had won it in 1984–85.

After the season was over, a writer walked up to Brad at his locker room seat and asked how he had made such a great improvement in his game. Without saying a word, Brad turned and pointed at Mark.

At one point during that season, the pairing did not allow a goal even-strength for five weeks. Five weeks! And McCrimmon was being too modest when he gave most of the credit to Howe because two years later McCrimmon, then with the Calgary Flames, led the league with a plus-48. That was the year the Flames, led by McCrimmon, first challenged for a Stanley Cup. A year later, the Flames broke up the Edmonton Oilers' dynasty by winning their first and only crown.

Brad and Mark were a big reason why we were able to make it to the Stanley Cup Final in 1985 and 1987. They just knew where the other was going to be and what territory had to be covered. Seldom were they caught out of position. They were roommates on the road, and you can be sure they weren't talking about the latest movie or the stock market when they went out to dinner. It was just hockey around the clock.

On some of the longer trips we enjoyed a couple days off. Players looked forward to going out on the town in places like Los Angeles, and because we were winning a lot, it made it easier for us to enjoy ourselves. After Ron Hextall won the Conn Smythe Trophy as the 1987 playoff MVP, he used his winnings to pay for a team party at a Mexican restaurant, complete with margaritas, etc. As expected, several players overindulged, and the obligatory rush to the bathroom (for relief through the facial portal) ensued.

Brad could drink a lot and almost never get sick. That only added to the legend.

When we were on the road, I could often be found in Brad and Mark's room. One time we were in Los Angeles, and we were coming off a couple days off. We filled the bathtub with enough beer to service a small army. After we won (which we knew we were going to do), we took advantage of that. Guys would wrestle one another, but Brad always beat me. He was strong as a mule. One time, we partied all night, even though some of the guys had an early tee time at Los Angeles Country Club. It was kind of a tough day for some of us. It's rather difficult to hit a golf ball when you can't see straight.

Brad could have had a longer stay with the Flyers, but a contract extension dispute spelled the end. It's hard to believe, but the two sides were only $35,000 apart. Philadelphia made the mistake of thinking he was going to eventually cave in, but knowing Brad, I knew that wasn't going to happen. He stuck by his guns, and it didn't take long for him to wind up in Calgary, which was a budding powerhouse. They basically gave him away to the Flames for a couple draft picks. It was probably the worst "non-signing" in the history of the Flyers. We never did as well after that, and it truly was a shame. Meanwhile, he went on to become the captain of the Flames in 1989–90. Remember, this was when the Oilers were still considered the powerhouse of the West and the Flames somehow made it through to the Final and defeated Montreal.

After playing for Boston, Philadelphia, and Calgary, Brad moved on to Detroit, then Hartford and Phoenix. The Hartford stop coincided with my last year in the NHL there. The thing I remember most about that stay was that Brad took budding superstar Chris Pronger under his wing. Brad taught him how to work out a little better and how to act, and he was a great role model for that.

I remember that season clearly because after Pronger scored his first NHL goal, I somehow wound up with his hockey stick. I asked him if he wanted to keep it, and he said he didn't, so I took it. I still have that. We got along pretty well. He assisted on my 1,000th NHL point later in the season. It was against the Flyers, no less.

By the time his career was over, Brad had partnered with such NHL greats as Boston's Bourque, Philadephia's Howe, Detroit's Nicklas Lidström, and Hartford's Chris Pronger. After that, Brad moved into coaching. He was an assistant coach for New York Islanders head coach Mike Milbury. That was followed by a tenure as head coach of the minor league Saskatoon Blades. His ambition was to become an NHL head coach, and he saw this move as a way to show he could run a bench. From there, it was on to assistant coaching positions with Calgary, Atlanta, and Detroit.

Then tragedy struck. In 2011, Brad made the fateful decision to accept the vacant coaching job with Russia's Lokomotiv Yaroslavl of the Kontinental Hockey League. At the very start of the season, on September 7, the Yaroslavl team plane crashed, and there were no survivors. Brad's life ended far too early at age 52.

When I heard the news, I was shocked. I will always remember that day. I considered myself one of his best friends. I knew his wife, Maureen, and his two kids. I talk with them a lot. I miss him all the time because he was such a great guy. He gave back; he had charities. I'll always remember him as a great leader, someone who loved to talk hockey. I'm glad he won the Cup in 1989 because he was the leader on that team, and he deserved it. For him, coaching was just another way to stay in the game and be a part of everything. It remains a painful memory, similar to Pelle's. They were both very special to me. And I miss them all to this day.

Brad was an unbelievable guy. I think about him every day, how much he meant to me. He had nicknames like "Sarge" and "Beast," but I just called him Brad, because I knew him and cared about him long before all the publicity of our careers.

CHAPTER 13

BAND OF (INJURED) BROTHERS

ALTHOUGH THE INCIDENTS happened nearly 35 years apart, they undoubtedly helped Mark Howe and me form an even stronger bond than the one we'd had prior to my stroke in September 2015. Mark had gone through a similar life-threatening injury of his own back on December 27, 1980, while playing for the Hartford Whalers. During a game that evening, Mark raced back into his defensive end for a puck, lost his balance, and went crashing into the net feet first. The cage lifted up, exposing the point in the back of the goal. It pierced his lower back, just missing his spinal column. A few inches over here or there and the story might have had a much more tragic ending.

During the game, the New York Islanders were coming in on a 3-on-2; Mark pivoted toward the net when he was accidentally bumped by John Tonelli, driving the lane. Mark's momentum took him into the net, flying into the piece of sheet metal that used to deflect pucks in the middle of the net. It all happened in a split second, but he knew enough to try to protect his bad back. So, while sliding on his back, he lifted his legs up so he could absorb the blow with his knees. Instead, the metal jammed five inches into his backside, just inches from what could have been real trouble.

Mark, as brave a guy as I've ever met, was terrified, and the look on his teammates' faces justified it. Mark was quickly losing blood and the outlook seemed rather bleak.

As it turned out, the metal protrusion slid right through Mark, nearly coming out of his hip. His father, Gordie, who had retired from the National Hockey League the season before after a Hall of Fame career, was at the game and hurried down from the stands to the trainer's room, where a doctor was grabbing Mark's feet to check for paralysis.

From what I remember, the recovery was grueling, as there were infections, fevers, and powerful medication that kept Mark practically bedridden. Similar to what I experienced after the stroke, his appetite was completely gone. After he had spent days in bed, doctors warned Mark that he needed to get up and walk. Every time he tried, he got sick. Finally, Gordie lifted him off the hospital bed and decided it was time for him to walk. And walk they did, because when your dad is Gordie Howe, you do what you're told.

Mark spent a month in and out of hospitals and returned to play 20 pounds lighter. He missed six weeks, but his game took much longer to return. One good thing to come out of it, at least from my perspective, was that he demanded a trade from the Whalers and eventually they acceded to his wishes.

I kind of know what he went through because of my experience. The medical people tell me I almost died from my stroke. It took a long time to come back from that. Like Mark, I learned there are no shortcuts with rehab. You have to put the work in every day. When you're faced with a serious health crisis, it's practically all-consuming.

That's how a team grows closer, because you get to know teammates' backgrounds and what makes them tick. It you know a guy's strengths and weaknesses in the thinking department, it makes it that much easier to know what his tendencies are. In a sport like hockey, you often have to react like the snap of a finger. Knowing what the other four position players on the ice are doing makes the process that much smoother.

This is particularly important in special teams play. On the power play, the whole idea is to find the guy who isn't being covered all that tightly so that he can get a decent shot on net. On give-and-go plays, it can make all the difference in the world. Ditto on the penalty kill. There's more to it than standing in one spot waving your stick around. If you can find a way to get in front of the big shooters and block a shot yourself, it makes it a heck of a lot easier for a goalie to do his job. You can worry about the black-and-blue marks later.

I remember the way the old nets were set up with the sharp points lodged in the back. They were an accident waiting to happen. In my mind, I knew from the outset they were dangerous. Mark was very scared at that time. In the hospital right after it happened, he asked his father if he was going to die.

Thankfully he recovered and became one of the best defensemen I ever played with or against. His skating stride was smooth and effortless. No doubt he inherited some of that from his famous father, who was the Wayne Gretzky of his generation. The horrible thing we have in common about the two health scares is the uncertainty factor. No medical person or specialist can say unequivocally if you're going to come out of the crisis in one piece. You just have to put in the work and hope/pray for the best.

We both have faith, and I can't stress enough how important that is. I think I can speak for him when I say we believe that God is more powerful than the rest of our lives. These are just reminders that faith makes a difference. You can pray, meditate, and just think about everything in a positive way and maybe that helps the recovery process.

Mark was always a great leader. He led by example, in the truest sense of the words. He didn't have to say much because his incredible play did most of the talking for him. Without a doubt, he's the best defenseman to ever wear a Flyers uniform. Playing alongside Brad McCrimmon was a bonus for both guys.

Those two guys were inseparable on and off the ice. Brad was proud of the duo's performances, including that 1985–86 season. On the road, the two of them roomed together, and I would make it a point to be in there as often as I could because the talk was nonstop and it was all about hockey. Mark and Brad had some great stories to tell. They remembered everything. I was a little different. When the game was over, I might take a couple things out of it, but the rest was history. I sort of went day by day and each day I tried to move forward.

They were especially great when we were on the road and won. There would be the "mandatory" post-game beers and small parties. That's where you caught up with everything that was going on, including the gossip.

No doubt the story about Mark crashing into the net came up a time or two. As time went by, a lot of us realized how life-changing that incident could have been. Maybe it already was. When you come out of a crash like that or a stroke like I had, I think it gives you a greater appreciation for life. You're more thankful for everything that we have.

Even though we're not together as much as we used to be, we still remain close. He's played in my celebrity hockey tournament to raise money for charity, and I hope to have him back again. He's looking to help wherever and whenever he can, and I would expect nothing less. That's the kind of guy that he is. He never asks for anything; he's very humble and shy. He should have been in the Hockey Hall of Fame when he was first eligible back in the late '90s, but it took all the way until 2011 for the voters to finally wake up and put him in that shrine.

I'm proud to be his friend.

CHAPTER 14

A KERR-IFIC TALENT

O F ALL THE PLAYERS I competed with or against during my NHL career, no one was more impressive than the soft-spoken, hard-shooting Tim Kerr.

To say he was a gentle giant might be an understatement because when he had a puck on his stick, he was anything but polite. No doubt more than one defender thought about skating for cover.

Looking back on his years with the Flyers, New York Rangers, and Hartford Whalers, it's pretty hard to believe he went undrafted. The Flyers signed him as a free agent in 1980 and after a few average seasons, he caught fire in 1983–84 and the rest, as they say, is history.

Tim was one of the best natural scorers I've ever shared the ice with. Starting in 1984, he put together four straight 50-goal seasons and set a record with 34 power-play goals in the 1983–84 campaign. I would say he's the best power-play competitor I've ever seen…and I've seen some great ones. He knew how to hit the holes. Even though defenders knew he was going to station himself in front of the net, there wasn't much they could do about it. You try moving a 6'3", 235-pound guy once he's set up shop.

As the years went by, he moved around a little bit more to make himself an easier target for teammates' passes. His quick, accurate release from the right flank often resulted in a goal. I remember back on April 13, 1985, Tim scored four goals in just over eight minutes to help us beat the New York Rangers in a series-clinching game.

Tim and I worked well together because we were so familiar with each other's moves. That's probably one of the reasons why we clicked on the power play. The idea on the power play is to get the puck moving quickly, either by fast passing or deception. If defenders tried to gang up on Tim, that left some other guys open for shots.

The expressions on the faces of the Rangers after that eight-minute rampage probably said it all. They couldn't believe how accurate or how fast the shots coming off Tim's stick were. Neither could we. Funny thing was, he really didn't do much in the way of a post-score celebration—maybe slightly raise his stick and crack a slight smile. Just another day at the office.

Tim's quiet way of doing business sort of rubbed off on other players. They accepted that old "act like you've been there before" line after scoring a goal. He had such great balance on his skates and was so composed in traffic—many viewed him as the perfect scoring machine. And he was darn close to it.

Around that time I was playing on a first line with Tim and captain Dave Poulin. Tim was a real quiet guy after practice. He didn't hang out all that much after games or practices. But he always was close by with the team on the road and would have the occasional beer with the guys. He was always busy. Tim had a lot of business deals going on. He worked with cars and owned a restaurant in Avalon, New Jersey, that he ran for a few years.

Ultimately, I believe Tim would have made the Hockey Hall of Fame if not for injuries. Even missing a lot of games, he managed to score 370 goals in 655 regular season games. In 1987, Tim's 58 goals (after overcoming an early season bout with meningitis) were second only to Wayne Gretzky's 62 for the NHL scoring crown. That's pretty rarefied air.

The most significant injury was probably one to his shoulder, which kept him out of the final two rounds of our run to the Stanley Cup Final in 1987. Boy, was he ever missed in that championship series against Gretzky, Messier, and the rest of the talented Edmonton Oilers. Even without him, we reached a Game 7 and even managed to take a 1–0 lead in the ultimate contest. Who knows? If Tim had been healthy and gotten a power-play goal or two, the outcome might have been different.

The Windsor, Ontario, native had to undergo a total of five shoulder operations over the next 14 months and things were never quite the same after that. Again, he was never the type to complain. Injuries are a part of hockey, and if you're going to go into the dirty areas, like Tim and I did, you can expect some damage to the body parts, some of it worse than others.

Who knows how good he could have been? He had to retire at age 33. That's far too early for any professional sport. It's likely he would have scored 500 goals if not for injuries in those later years. But even with all that working against him, he bounced back from the shoulder problems in the 1988–89 season to score 48 goals in just 69 games, and that won him the Bill Masterton Memorial Trophy for perseverance and dedication to the sport of hockey. I can't think of a worthier recipient.

As courageous as Tim was on the ice, he was equally impressive off it. On October 16, 1990, his wife, Kathy, fell victim to a fast-spreading infection after giving birth to their daughter Kimberly and suddenly died. It was a difficult time for him and, to a degree, everyone in the Flyers organization. But he didn't say much about it. He pretty much stayed to himself and did his own thing. I admire him for that.

Tim started his own road race in Avalon, New Jersey, and it was a big success right off the bat. It's become a classic event at the Jersey Shore. And that's where he met his current wife, Midge. They have two sons and three daughters.

Through the years I've gotten to know Tim pretty well. It's safe to say he was—and is—a role model to a lot of people, both in hockey as well as outside the sport. There are lots of impressive stats out there, like his second-best all-time playoff shooting percentage of 20.3. But the one thing that will stay with me is his emotional strength. They often talk about which person you would like to have in a foxhole with you during combat. Need I say more?

CHAPTER 15

BOSTON BOUND

AFTER AN UNEXPECTED RUN to the conference finals in 1988–89, the Flyers were at a bit of a crossroads. Although the team still had a number of star forwards in their mid-twenties, such as Rick Tocchet and Murray Craven, a number of core offensive players were either at or headed into their landmark thirties years.

That list included Ilkka Sinisalo, 31; Keith Acton, 31; Ken Linseman, 31; Dave Poulin, 30; and myself, 30. Tim Kerr, 29, was right behind us. So our general manager, Bob Clarke, had some tough decisions to make. He could either hang on to some of these guys who had been instrumental in trips to the 1985 and 1987 Stanley Cup Finals or start making some deals and prepare for the next generation of stars in the making.

Incredibly, the Flyers had made the Stanley Cup playoffs in 18 consecutive seasons dating back to 1971–72. That run of success included two Stanley Cups (1974, 1975) plus three more trips to the Final (1980, 1985, 1987). But things got off to a slow start in the 1989–90 campaign, and rumors were flying.

Poulin, our incredibly gifted captain, was the first to go. He had been the leader of our special teams, especially on penalty killing. Who can forget the three-on-five goal he scored against the Quebec Nordiques in a 1985 Stanley Cup semifinal game?

Injuries slowed Poulin a bit at the start of the 1989–90 season and his play deteriorated so much that he was stripped of the team captaincy (which went to Ron Sutter) in December. A month later he was headed north to Boston in exchange for ex-Flyers center Ken Linseman.

There were a lot of whispers about me, too. I was still making a decent contribution, but the Flyers made it known they were in selling mode as their chances of making the playoffs faded. The Flyers would go on to finish dead last in the Patrick Division and be one of just five teams not to make the playoffs. The Bruins had already acquired half of the Flyers' top two forward penalty-killers when they dealt for Poulin, so why not complete the set? So I was off to Boston in exchange for a second-round pick in the 1990 NHL Draft on March 2.

Even though I had sensed my days in Philadelphia were over, it didn't make it any easier to leave the Flyers. At the time of the deal I was getting over hand surgery. Looking back, I think Clarke did me a favor, because the Bruins were the top-seeded team in the East and the Flyers were about to miss the postseason for the first time in a generation.

Besides that, I was about to be a free agent, so here was a chance to show that I still had it when the playoffs rolled around. Having Dave already on the Bruins helped the transition. We were considered two of the NHL's best penalty-killers of the '80s, and that made this reunion that much more special. Plus, we were joining a team featuring future Hall of Famers Ray Bourque and Cam Neely.

Let me add, it wasn't easy leaving the Flyers, at least from an emotional standpoint. I had grown attached to Philadelphia and its great hockey fans. I might as well have had a tattoo of the Flyers logo etched into one of my shoulders. Lots of good times, lots of memories.

You couldn't have scripted my first goal with the Bruins any better. We were playing at the old Boston Garden, and I scored shorthanded. The place went nuts. That's when I knew I was going to fit in there just fine.

Things continued to go well in Beantown. The Bruins won the Presidents' Trophy for league supremacy with 101 points. In addition to Neely up front, they had Craig Janney, Bob Sweeney, and Bobby Carpenter. There were not many superstars but a whole lot of role players who knew how the game worked.

Even though the Bruins were highly rated, the road to the Final was not easy. It took seven games to put away the Hartford Whalers. Bourque was hurt for a couple of those games and that left the boys from Connecticut—including Ron Francis, Kevin Dineen, and Dave Tippett—a lot of room to operate. But we managed to prevail when Bourque made an inspirational return for Game 7 and helped us win a heated rivalry in the deciding contest.

Next up: the vaunted Montreal Canadiens. This was a series in which Poulin and I figured rather prominently. It seemed like the Bruins were having problems with Montreal all the time. Having the two of us as leaders really made a difference, especially on the penalty kill. We might have lost half a step by then, but we were schooled enough to know where to be and get in the proper lanes to block passes and shots. Both of us had figured prominently in the 1987 Cup semifinal win over the Canadiens.

If anyone thought there was going to be a letdown in the East finals against Washington, they were sadly mistaken. The Bruins' offense really clicked in that series and the defense was close to impeccable. The 4–0 series outcome was almost predictable.

Things changed drastically when we took on the playoff-tested Edmonton Oilers in the Stanley Cup Final. Even though Wayne Gretzky was long gone to Los Angeles, the Oilers still had the services of such talents as Mark Messier, Jari Kurri, Glenn Anderson, and Paul Coffey. We knew it wasn't going to be easy, but no one could have predicted the epic battle right off the bat in Game 1. For one thing, the lights went out during the game, leaving everyone in the dark for nearly half an hour. And then, in the third overtime, Petr Klíma turned out our lights for the winning goal.

Somehow that took a lot of the wind out of our sails. The Oilers, winners of four Stanley Cups in the '80s, made it a fifth in 1990. Losing that first game really sapped some of our confidence. Even though we won the first game in Edmonton, we were running out of gas. Edmonton would go on to sweep the next two games for its fifth Cup since 1984. Oilers goaltender Bill Ranford won the Conn Smythe Trophy for MVP and justifiably so. He played unbelievably. It was tough to get one by him, so I imagine the vote was close to unanimous.

Without a doubt, I was hoping to stay with Boston and maybe sign a new contract with them. At 31, I thought I still had a lot of hockey left. But it didn't seem like Bruins general manager Harry Sinden wanted to offer me too much. Right around then I found out that the Flyers had fired GM Bob Clarke. This was just the first time the Flyers had missed the playoffs in Clarke's seven years at the helm, but team owner Ed Snider had passed the decision-making torch to his son, Jay, so No. 16 was out.

But not entirely out of the NHL. Clarke quickly landed on his feet in Minnesota, taking over the North Stars operation. When Clarke found out I was not getting much interest in Boston, he brought me to the Twin Cities as a free agent. So I signed with them for three years.

The whole thing couldn't have worked out better. In my first year in the Land of 10,000 Lakes, I put up 73 points. That was good enough for third on the team behind only Dave Gagner and Brian Bellows and well ahead of established stars such as Neal Broten and Bobby Smith.

Those of us in the locker room thought we might have something special going on. But a lot of people really didn't believe in us. In fact, hardly anybody picked us to get past the Presidents' Trophy–winning Chicago Blackhawks in the first round. They had finished the season with 106 points, and we had just 68. In fact, our 27–39–14 mark in the regular season was nothing to write home about.

Somehow we skated past the Blackhawks by a comfortable 4–2 mark. If memory serves me correctly, I won Game 1 with an overtime goal in Chicago. That has to be one of the highlight goals of my career. That goal really made a difference in our overall confidence. We figured if we could beat the mighty Blackhawks on their home ice, we could beat anybody. I would have to say it was a pretty special moment for me.

But we were just getting started. Next in line were the St. Louis Blues, who were seeded second. Our coach, Bob Gainey, had been one of the best checking forwards in the history of the NHL and knew a little something about shutting down opponents' offenses. So he decided to put Gaétan Duchesne on a checking line and that worked out just fine against the Blues' top scorer, Brett Hull. The son of hockey legend Bobby Hull had his hands full trying to elude that defensive wave.

After vanquishing the Blues, it was time to face some tougher competition, namely the five-time Stanley Cup champion Edmonton Oilers. Boy, I just couldn't elude these guys in the postseason. I had played them in 1985 and 1987 with the Flyers, in 1990 with Boston, and now 1991 with Minnesota. Only this time, I finally finished on the winning side of things.

Of course, Edmonton gave its usual all-in effort, led by its gritty captain, the indomitable Mark Messier. He and I had crossed paths more than a few times. What a leader. This turned out to be his last hurrah in Edmonton. While Wayne Gretzky is generally acknowledged as the driving force in the Oilers' dynasty, Mark was the workhorse in the corners and the dirty areas. One look at his 25-year career numbers—1,756 games, 694 goals, 1,193 assists, 1,887 points—and you can see why he deserves to be mentioned in the same sentence with Gretzky, Mario Lemieux, Bobby Hull, Gordie Howe, Bobby Orr, and others. How about an amazing 109 goals and 295 points in his postseason career?

It was his focus that impressed so many on both his team and the other. Plus, he was as crafty and imaginative as they come. How many times did he win an offensive-zone faceoff, rush to the net, and create havoc in front of the goalie, eventually resulting in a goal? He finished his career with a plus-211 and six Stanley Cups, including some of his finest work with the New York Rangers when they won it all in 1994.

We played well in all aspects of the game, including special teams. Our power play was sharp and converting at crucial times in the game. We may have caught the Oilers a little bit by surprise.

After all that work, we still had to face the mighty Pittsburgh Penguins, and for us, it just wasn't to be. They had the already legendary Lemieux but also a strong supporting cast. I'm not sure if we were intimidated, exactly, because we won the first game. They had goalie Tom Barrasso, Paul Coffey, Joey Mullen, Larry Murphy, Mark Recchi, and Bryan Trottier. Eventually that depth proved too much for us to overcome. They would go on to win the Cup again in 1992 over my old coach, Mike Keenan, and the Chicago Blackhawks.

I was satisfied with my play in the 1991 playoffs. Eight of my goals came on the power play and overall, I scored 23 points in 23 games. I don't have to look in a book to remember those numbers. In the Chicago series, I scored a goal on goalie Dominik Hašek for what proved to be the game-winner. Also, that goal moved me past Bobby Hull to first place among left wings on the all-time playoff scoring list (April 12, 1991).

The next couple years some injuries slowed me down. I wound up getting traded to Hartford, took a brief sabbatical to play in Lagano, Switzerland, and helped win the 1993 Spengler Cup while over there.

I wanted one more season in the NHL to achieve some milestones, so I returned to the United States and signed a one-year free-agent contract with the Whalers. Everything worked out fine. I played in my 1,000th NHL game. The game was in Hartford; we were playing against the Los Angeles Kings. Having Gretzky on the ice was really special. My old coach in Philly, Paul Holmgren, was running the show there, so it was a comfortable fit. I also wanted to get my 1,000th point and guess who it came against? The Flyers.

How much better does it get than to score your 1,000th point on a two-goal night at your old rink, the Spectrum? Judging from the sound of the applause, a lot of people were pulling for me to achieve that special number, even though it came at the expense of their team. And would you believe that game knocked the Flyers out of the playoffs? I'm not saying I took any special joy in that, but deep down it did give me a bit of satisfaction.

Propp's rookie shot with the Flyers, 1979. (Bruce Bennett Studios via Getty Images Studios/Getty Images)

Propp with the Flyers in 1987. (Bruce Bennett Studios via Getty Images Studios/Getty Images)

Propp taking a face-off with the Flyers, 1982.

Propp in action in long pants, 1982. (Focus on Sport/Getty Images)

Propp's penalty shot goal in 1983 against the Vancouver Canucks' Ken Ellacott.

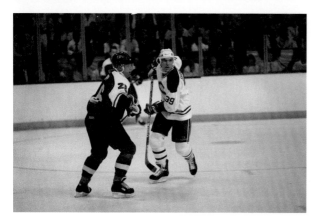

Propp playing against the Canadiens in the conference finals, 1989. (Denis Brodeur/ NHLI via Getty Images)

Propp with Howie Mandell at an Atlantic City Casino in 1990.

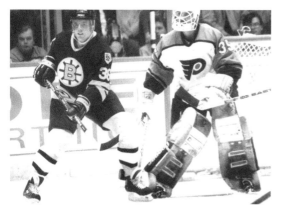

Propp, as a Boston Bruin, playing against the Flyers in 1990.

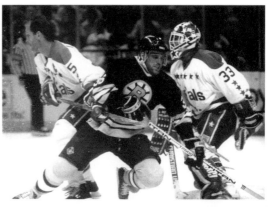

Propp with the Boston Bruins in the 1990 playoffs against the Washington Capitals.

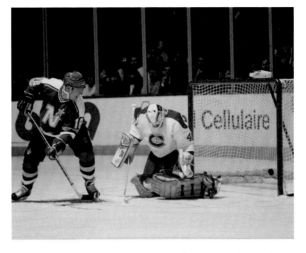

Propp with the North Stars against the Montreal Canadiens, 1991. (Denis Brodeur/NHLI via Getty Images)

Propp's Minnesota North Stars headshot, 1991.

Propp in action with the North Stars in 1991.

Propp playing with the North Stars in 1992.

Propp, Evander Holyfield,
and Scott McKay in 1992.

Propp's Hartford Whalers card from
1994.

Propp with the Hartford Whalers in
1994.

Propp scored his 1,000[th] point against the Flyers
in 1994.

HARTFORD WHALERS
VS
BUFFALO SABRES
Wednesday, February 16, 1994

General Manager: Paul Holmgren; **Head Coach:** Pierre McGuire; **Director of Player Personnel:** Kevin Maxwell; **Assistant Coaches:** Kevin McCarthy, Paul Gillis; **Strength and Conditioning Coach:** Doug McKenney; **Goaltending Instructor:** Steve Weeks; **Medical Trainer:** Bud Gouveia; **Equipment Manager:** Skip Cunningham; **Assistant Equipment Managers:** Bob Gorman, Todd MacGowan

President: Seymour H. Knox III; **Executive Vice President of Sports Operations:** Gerry Meehan; **Head Coach and General Manager:** John Muckler; **Assistant Coaches:** John Tortorella, D Lever; **Trainers:** Jim Pizzutelli, Rip Simonick

POS.	NO.	PLAYER	GP	G	A	PTS	+/-	PIM
D	3	ZALAPSKI, Zarley	47	7	25	32	-2	50
D	4	PATRICK, James	43	6	18	24	-3	30
D	5	GODYNYUK, Alexander	51	2	19	21	19	49
D	6	BURT, Adam	57	1	17	18	-3	73
L	7	CUNNEYWORTH, Randy	52	9	6	15	-1	83
C	8	SANDERSON, Geoff	55	31	16	47	-5	24
D	10	McCRIMMON, Brad	40	1	3	4	0	42
R	14	SANDLAK, Jim	27	6	2	8	6	32
R	15	*HARKINS, Todd	7	0	0	0	-3	13
R	16	VERBEEK, Pat	57	27	24	51	-6	129
L	18	KRON, Robert	57	18	19	37	2	6
C	21	CASSELS, Andrew	56	7	30	37	-8	31
C	22	JANSSENS, Mark	57	2	6	8	-8	95
L	24	*STORM, Jim	42	6	8	14	7	10
L	26	PROPP, Brian	42	9	9	18	2	40
D	27	MARCHMENT, Bryan	52	4	11	15	-14	153
R	29	POTVIN, Marc	38	1	2	3	-7	231
C	32	CHIBIREV, Igor	29	4	11	15	8	2
D	44	*PRONGER, Chris	57	3	18	21	6	77
L	51	*SMYTH, Kevin	6	1	0	1	1	2
C	92	NYLANDER, Michael	48	8	29	37	1	16

POS.	NO.	PLAYER	GP	G	A	PTS	+/-	P
D	5	MUNI, Craig	55	1	10	11	22	
D	7	SVOBODA, Petr	46	1	13	14	6	
D	8	BODGER, Doug	50	4	21	25	8	
C	10	HAWERCHUK, Dale	54	24	35	59	9	
L	13	KHMYLEV, Yuri	50	16	19	35	9	
C	14	HANNAN, Dave	56	2	6	8	-1	
L	15	*PETRENKO, Sergei	12	0	3	3	-3	
C	17	*SIMON, Todd	1	0	0	0	0	
R	18	PRESLEY, Wayne	38	10	4	14	10	
L	19	WOOD, Randy	57	13	16	29	5	
C	20	SWEENEY, Bob	47	9	12	21	-1	
D	24	MOLLER, Randy	53	0	4	4	-4	1
C	26	*PLANTE, Derek	52	18	25	43	6	
L	27	MAY, Brad	57	13	18	31	-5	1
R	28	AUDETTE, Donald	52	17	20	37	1	
D	29	*TSYGUROV, Denis	7	0	0	0	-1	
L	32	RAY, Rob	55	2	4	6	2	2
L	36	*BARNABY, Matthew	24	2	4	6	-7	
C	40	BLACK, James	15	2	3	5	-4	
D	41	SUTTON, Ken	52	2	16	18	-5	
D	42	SMEHLIK, Richard	57	12	13	25	10	
L	43	*DAWE, Jason	7	1	2	3	2	
R	89	MOGILNY, Alexander	44	24	31	55	12	

NO.	GOALTENDER	GPI	MINS	AVG	W-L-T
1	BURKE, Sean	26	1573	2.59	11-12-3
30	REESE, Jeff	13	705	3.40	4- 5-2

NO.	GOALTENDER	GPI	MINS	AVG	W-L
31	FUHR, Grant	19	1073	4.03	7- 9
39	HASEK, Dominik	41	2374	2.00	20-15

*Indicates a Rookie

M.D. HEALTH PLAN
THREE STAR AWARD

PLAYER	STAR NUMBER 1	2	3	=	3-STAR TOTAL
1. S. Burke (G)	3	5	5	=	35
2. P. Verbeek	4	4	2	=	34
3. G. Sanderson	4	1	2	=	25
4. R. Kron	2	3	2	=	21
5. M. Nylander	2	3	0	=	19
6. F. Pietrangelo (G)	2	1	3	=	16
J. Reese (G)	2	2	0	=	16
8. B. Propp	1	1	0	=	8
9. R. Cunneyworth	1	0	1	=	6
A. Godynyuk	1	0	1	=	6
11. I. Chibirev	1	0	0	=	5
12. C. Pronger	0	1	1	=	4
J. Storm	0	1	1	=	4
J. Patrick	0	1	1	=	4
15. M. Janssens	0	1	0	=	3
A. Cassels	0	0	3	=	3
17. Z. Zalapski	0	0	1	=	1
A. Burt	0	0	1	=	1
TEAM TOTALS	**23**	**24**	**24**	**=**	**211**

(Five points for 1st star, 3 for 2nd, 1 for 3rd)

ITT HARTFORD
TOP GUN AWARD
(THROUGH 57 GAMES)

PLAYER	TOTAL POINT
Pat Verbeek	51 (27-24-5
Geoff Sanderson	47 (31-16-4
Robert Kron	37 (18-19-3
Michael Nylander	37 (8-29-3

$1,000 is awarded by ITT Hartford to the favorite charities of the first half point leader, $1,000 to the second half point leader and $2,000 to the top scorer for the entire season.

Photography by Diane Sobolewski

Hartford Whalers vs. Buffalo Sabres card, February 16, 1994.

Brian Propp at the Plus-Minus Awards with Darcy Rota.

Propp being inducted into the Flyers Hall of Fame in 1999. (Bruce Bennett Studios via Getty Images Studios/Getty Images)

Propp with Ben Crenshaw, designer of the Hidden Creek Golf Course, in Egg Harbor City, New Jersey, in 2002.

Bobby Orr, Propp, Denis Potvin, Guy LaFleur, and Brian Kilrea, cigar aficionados, 1999.

Propp and Joe Pesci at a celebrity golf event at Blue Heron Pines, 2006.

Propp with Gordie Howe and Mark Howe at a Flyers alumni golf tournament, 2015.

Propp playing in the Global Hockey Legends For Hurricane Sandy Relief Charity Game on April 13, 2013, in Newark, New Jersey. (Andy Marlin/AM Photography/ Getty Images)

Propp playing in the Philadelphia–Pittsburgh alumni game in 2017. (Credit: Bill McCay)

Propp playing against Pittsburgh in 2017. (Credit: Bill McCay)

Propp doing the Guffaw against Pittsburgh in 2017. (Credit: Bill McCay)

The Philadelphia–Pittsburgh alumni team photo in 2017. (Credit: Bill McCay)

Propp and Bernie Parent as Flyers ambassadors, 2018.

CHAPTER 16

TRADE OF THE CENTURY

W HEN IT COMES TO hockey trades, they don't get any bigger than the one involving the Flyers and the former Quebec Nordiques (now Colorado Avalanche) in June 1992. The question is, who got the best of the deal? Eric Lindros turned out to be a great player for the Flyers, but Peter Forsberg was equally proficient for the Nordiques. As for the final Stanley Cup scoreboard, albeit with very different team roster casts: Forsberg 2, Lindros 0.

The Flyers, desperate to end a three-year playoff drought (which would eventually become five), attempted to pull off a blockbuster deal for consensus 1991 No. 1 pick Lindros, who had been taken with the top choice by the Canadian club. Forget about the 15 million bucks or the top draft picks or the busload of players the Nordiques wanted in return. The one they really had their eyes on was young Swedish star Forsberg, who had been taken by the Flyers at No. 6 in the 1991 draft.

The only problem was the New York Rangers also had an intense desire to acquire Lindros and had a package of players and draft slots equal to or better than the Flyers. Since it happened more than 30 years ago, there's no need for me to go over it again piece by piece. Here's what you need to know: Lindros refused to play for the Nordiques and owner Marcel Aubut and sat out for a year. The Flyers offered Forsberg along with another first-rounder (1990) Mike Ricci, goaltender Ron Hextall, forward Chris Simon, defensemen Steve Duchesne and Kerry Huffman, future first-round picks (1993, '94), and the aforementioned cash. The Nordiques agreed to that deal but also one by the Rangers, so arbitrator Larry Bertuzzi had to make a ruling, which came out in favor of the Flyers on June 30.

I was still playing at the time, having just completed my second year with the North Stars and getting ready to split the 1992–93 season between Minnesota and Lugano of the Swiss-A League. My first impression of Lindros was that he was immature at the start, sort of like me in my first couple years in the NHL. He just did what his mom and dad asked him to do. I didn't talk much, and I really didn't know what was going on. It just took me some time to learn from the best, including Clarke. Other guys I studied closely included Howe, Poulin, and McCrimmon.

If you look at everything in the rearview mirror, it's easy to second-guess every move that was made. If, and it's a big if, the Flyers had hung on to Forsberg, it might have enhanced their chances of winning a Stanley Cup, because Peter made all the players around him better. Lindros could have turned into a player like that, and if he had known better, things might have turned out differently. He could have learned a lot and won a little bit more. He had to learn to be a leader and know how to win a Stanley Cup. That's what they got him for.

Forsberg was such a good player and more aware of what was going on. Just look at the goal he scored in a shootout on goaltender Corey Hirsch in the 1994 Winter Olympic Games in Lillehammer, Norway. Forsberg basically passed the puck from his left-side forehand to his right-side back hand and shoveled the puck into the net in one motion. The arena went crazy. That's the kind of skill and out-of-the-box thinking he possessed. That goal won the gold medal for his native Sweden.

When Clarke returned to the Flyers for a second go-round as GM of the team in 1994–95, his contentious relationship with Lindros (which included his parents) certainly didn't help the situation. The failure in the 1997 Stanley Cup Final against Detroit, which the Red Wings won in a four-game sweep, spotlighted the fact the Flyers were a divided team. Coach Terry Murray calling it a "choking" situation once the Flyers were down 3–0 in the series simply amplified what everyone knew.

Fact is, Lindros had star power and he knew it. He went about his business without much outside interference. The Flyers had put so much into the trade to acquire Lindros that the 1996 Colorado Avalanche (formerly the Nordiques) and Forsberg cruised to the Stanley Cup that season. That only made the public relations situation back in Philadelphia an even worse nightmare.

It would take another few years for the situation to be resolved, with Lindros sitting out a season and then getting traded to the New York Rangers for several promising players. Forsberg would go on to win another Cup with the Avalanche, which only made the wounds a little bit harder to heal.

On the other hand, Lindros was no slouch. He won the NHL's Hart Memorial Trophy in 1995 as Most Valuable Player and his career scoring efficiency remains in the top 20 all-time at better than a point per game. As for Forsberg, he might have put in an even better career if not for problems with his feet, which affected his skating. The Swede still put up some remarkable numbers. He knew how to pass the puck and anticipated where players were going to be, à la Gretzky.

So, it's very difficult to take one side of the debate and justify it as being better. The Flyers needed someone like Lindros to get them out of their non-playoff rut. Within five years they were in the Stanley Cup Final, and although they lost to Detroit in four straight games after the 1997 season, they were respectable once again. Maybe if the Flyers had held onto Forsberg, they would have won a Cup. But they just didn't want to wait that long. They wanted something immediately. The debate goes on and it shows no signs of letting up.

————————

If you ask me, I would say one of the least appreciated aspects of professional ice hockey might very well be the science of amateur/ pro scouting, especially keeping an eye on all the young prospects around the world. After all, a general manager might pick up a key player through a trade or free agency, but the future success of most teams is based on which handful of 18-year-olds among hundreds is called to the stage when a given team is announced at the annual NHL draft.

The Flyers have made a concerted effort in recent years to make sure all their bases are covered, particularly with qualified people. Most of these scouts either played in the NHL or have been around the game so long they pretty much know what characteristics go into making a youngster a bona fide prospect for the NHL someday.

To that end, Philadelphia added former NHL star player Dany Heatley to its staff at the start of the 2023–24 season. Heatley had put together an exceptional if not controversial NHL career, which included stops in Atlanta, Ottawa, San Jose, Minnesota, and Anaheim. He reached the 50-goal and 100-point season milestones twice and made multiple All-Star teams. Having played with and against some of the best players in the early 21st century, Heatley knows some of the traits that go into making a competitive, well-rounded player.

Heatley went through a lot during his pro career, including the accidental death of Atlanta teammate Dan Snyder during a car accident in which Heatley was the driver. Although he did not receive any prison time, Heatley's one unfortunate moment followed him around for a long time.

It's my belief Heatley can relate well with today's younger players and what they have to go through. That can be either an 18-year-old prospect who is at the top of the charts or perhaps a slightly older kid who might have fallen through the cracks but still shows a lot of promise.

I'm familiar with a number of Flyers scouts, including the recently retired Al Hill, Ross Fitzpatrick (who played parts of several seasons for the Flyers), and Dave Brown, one of the most intimidating players in local hockey history. They all kind of know what goes into the makeup of a character player. They spent a lot of time in the game and watch players at all levels of play to see if they fit into the Flyers' style. They know what the team is looking for.

On the flip side of this, younger players are well aware they're being watched. When Sidney Crosby became eligible for the draft the year after the 2004–05 NHL lockout, there were armies of scouts filing reports. At the 1979 Memorial Cup Final between my team, the Brandon Wheat Kings, and the Peterborough Petes, there were scouts all over the place. There were 10 Brandon players drafted later that year, including Brad McCrimmon and Ray Allison. During the Memorial Cup games, every move was scrutinized. These were some of the best players in the junior ranks and many were in the "can't-miss" category. It was just a matter of what team was going to take a certain player and how high up in the draft order.

In those years, some kids might not have gotten as much attention as they do today. You can thank the internet and advanced technology for that. A youngster could play in Siberia and there's still going to be a file on him.

Every time a player goes undrafted and then makes it to the NHL, scouting comes under a bit of fire. In recent years the Flyers have had two young defensemen—Philippe Myers and Egor Zamula—who were not drafted and still found their way onto an NHL rink.

Here are some other undrafted players you might have heard of who eventually played for the Flyers and did rather well: Bernie Parent, Tim Kerr, Dave Poulin, Ed Van Impe, Gary Dornhoefer, and Joe Watson. You could practically start an All-Star team with that bunch.

Some kids might try to bring attention to themselves by conversing with scouts, but that wasn't me. I let my shooting do the talking. Probably the best way to put it—I was shy and didn't have a whole lot to say.

In the past there might have been a strong emphasis on skill and what someone could do with the puck. That has changed. I know the Flyers and other teams are looking for character. Of course, skill, the competitive level, and the role a player fits into all factor into the evaluation process. High up on the list is how well a player listens to his coaches. An added bonus might be how popular a player figures to be in the locker room. In my day, teammate Lindsay Carson was an exceptional utility player because he was very funny and could get teammates to laugh. Glen Cochrane also was also very good at getting people to crack up. Craig Berube was one of the best because of his usual stern demeanor—what they call a "straight man" in the humor business. These guys were wizards at lightening up a tense locker room.

Maybe the best at this was Keith Jones, who was (and is) the king of sarcasm. He was a fine player and actually spent some time on the old "Legion of Doom" line with Eric Lindros and

John LeClair. But one of his most natural personality traits was his quick wit and ability to get under opponents' skin with his razor-sharp observations. No doubt scouts saw some of that when they turned in their evaluations on him prior to the draft.

I should also mention a good scouting story about my former teammate and later GM, Bob Clarke.

Clarke played junior hockey back in his native Flin Flon, Manitoba, and had been diagnosed in his teens as diabetic. In those days, that sort of thing was deemed a red flag. As it turns out, nobody wanted to risk a first-round pick on the talented lad. But Flyers scout Gerry Melnyk must have seen something in Clarke that others didn't. After Clarke fell to the second round, Melnyk was determined to secure him. He called a diabetes specialist in Philadelphia who said Clarke would be fine if he looked after his health.

Melnyk then got back on the telephone and called Flyers general manager Bud Poile and convinced him to take Clarke with the second pick. As soon as that happened, both Montreal and Detroit called Poile with trade offers that included proven veteran players. To his credit, with Melnyk's whispers echoing in his ears, Poile said no to both proposals and made it clear Clarke was not for sale.

After watching Clarke serve as captain on two Stanley Cup championship teams and winning the NHL's MVP award three times, I would have to say Gerry the scout knew what he was talking about.

CHAPTER 17

GOING OUT IN STYLE

I ALWAYS HAD THE FEELING (or hope) that I was going to spend my entire career with the Flyers. But the team's long run of success going back to the early '70s was coming to an end. That led to my midseason trade to the Boston Bruins in 1990.

The next five years were tumultuous, to say the least. I wound up playing for Boston, Minnesota, and the former Hartford Whalers, not to mention two teams in Europe: HC Lugano (Switzerland) and Anglet (France). And did I mention the Spengler Cup, playing for Team Canada, during the 1992–93 season?

When all was said and done, my NHL numbers compared favorably with just about any top forward who ever came down the road. I wound up playing in 1,016 games, scored 425 goals, and added 579 assists for 1,004 points. Getting to that 1,000 mark for both points and games was important to me, which is why I wanted to play one more season with the Whalers in 1993–94.

The best years of my career, of course, were with the Flyers. I played 790 regular season games for the Orange, Black, and White. My 369 goals and 480 assists for 849 points stood third for a long time on the team's all-time scoring list, behind only Bob Clarke and Bill Barber, until Claude Giroux recently passed everyone but Clarke with 900 points.

I'm pretty proud of my Flyers playoff numbers as well. I played in 116 games with 52 goals and 60 assists for 112 points. For my career, if you include Boston, Minnesota, and Hartford, I registered 64 goals, 84 assists, and 148 points in 160 games. If you look at the big picture, in the 1980s I was 10th overall in NHL points with 55 game-winning goals and 20 shorthanded goals. I also share the Flyers' record for most shorthanded goals in a season (seven) with Mark Howe and Mike Richards.

Another number I won't forget is my plus/minus number, which is plus-298. That ranks No. 10 for all forwards in the history of the sport.

Plus/minus can be a rather subjective statistic in hockey because so much depends on how your teammates are playing. You can be having the game of your life, wind up on the short end of a 6–0 score, and, defensively, be responsible for maybe only a goal or two. But then you look at the post-game stat sheet and a big minus-3 is staring you right in the face. It can be a humbling—and somewhat irritating—experience.

On the flip side, there is no doubt my career plus-298 had a lot to do with playing on some great defensive teams in Philadelphia. You had guys who took a lot of pride in not getting scored upon, as well as players who didn't mind adding on a few extra goals when games got out of hand.

When your agent goes in to negotiate a new contract, it doesn't hurt to be coming off a plus-40 season. I managed to break the 40 mark four times in my career, including a plus-45 my rookie year. For sure, just being on the ice with a team that went 35 games without a loss in 1979–80 helped account for that lofty statistic. Playing hard at both ends of the rink can be a source of pride, too. Don't let any player tell you he's not thrilled when his team shuts out an opponent. Offensive numbers like five, six, or seven goals for a team in a game can be a lot of fun, but a shutout is perfection. It usually means your goalie gave a special performance and the rest of the team chipped in by putting the brakes on the other team's sharpshooters.

During the 1992–93 season, I had a chance to play in Europe, first with HC Lugano. Andy Murray was the coach there. He had been an assistant coach with the Flyers in my last year there and then I worked for him again when he moved over to the North Stars in 1991. So we had a good relationship. In my 24 games with HC Lugano, I still had something left in the tank, picking up 21 goals and 27 points. They weren't big on giving out assists, but that wasn't a big concern—the team just wanted goals.

For the three months in Switzerland, it was a blast. While we were there, I jumped into the Spengler Cup. Murray was the Team Canada coach. He was the head coach of the team six times in the tournament and won every one of them! The tournament was held in Davos, Switzerland, over the Christmas break and the level of play was pretty high. It was special because I got a chance to play for my native country.

I was the oldest player on the team. One of the youngest? Future Flyers defenseman Chris Therien, who was barely old enough to drink. Also on that team were NHL regulars Brian Savage and Morris Lukowich. It was really special. The tournament was played up in the mountains, so you couldn't ask for a better hockey setting. And this gave me a chance to display my leadership skills. I was in my thirties by then and had been to the Stanley Cup Final five times. That pretty much gave me instant respect. I showed I still had it by scoring three goals in three games. I can't even begin to tell you how special it was to take home a gold medal for Canada. Needless to say, I was very excited to be part of that.

Once things wrapped up with the Whalers following the 1993–94 season, I returned to Europe to play for HC Anglet. They played their games right near the France-Spain border, in the Pyrenees Mountains. What a place. Right on the ocean, it was a sight to be seen. We only played a couple games a week, which was fine with me. They even took three weeks off for Christmas. They gave us a car, an apartment, the full celebrity treatment. I really enjoyed my time there; a great way to end my hockey career. On the ice, I could still put the puck in the net, scoring 32 goals in 27 games. I should mention I did get suspended one time because I slashed a guy.

All the guys on the team had other jobs, so we practiced later in the day. We usually had Mondays off. I wouldn't go so far as to say it was a country-club atmosphere, but compared to the NHL it was a walk in the park.

So it was kind of nice to enjoy the travel. Spain was only about a half hour away. By the midpoint of the season, we were the top team in the league. But that meant a little bit more travel. So it was sort of like North American minor league hockey travel. There were 10-hour bus rides to Paris, but there wasn't a whole lot of complaining. And who could really gripe when we were served wine in the pregame meals? Now that was different. Those European teams know how to do it right!

It was just a fun, fun time for me. The town we were situated in was a little like Ocean City, New Jersey. A lot of people visited the area in the summer and then things quieted down in the winter. You couldn't ask for a better place to wrap up a hockey career.

CHAPTER 18

THE PUCK STOPS HERE

T HERE'S A TIME LIMIT attached to every player's career, some
longer than others. No doubt genetics can play a role in just
how long someone can keep their skates moving at NHL speed.
Lifestyle has something to say about it, too. If you don't have an
effective health regimen, chances are you're probably not going to
play too much past age 30. The grains in the hourglass simply run
out a little faster and before you know it, it's over.

Injuries, especially the major ones, also factor into the equa-
tion. One or two alone probably won't shorten your stay in the
big time, but a bunch of them can. By age 35, the cumulative
effect of a variety of health issues had ganged up on me and
begun to detract from my performances. Yet I was driven by a
number of incentives, the most significant being getting to those
1,000-point/1,000-game milestones. Along the way I had suffered a
significant eye injury that sidelined me for a while. A knee injury
knocked me out of action for 26 games. Then I messed up a hand
and that cost me another 27. One of the most painful problems
was a dislocated shoulder that affected my performances long
after I was cleared to play near the end of my career in 1994. If
your shoulders aren't working properly, it's tough to play hockey
at its highest level.

Keeping all that in mind, I was still chugging along pretty well toward the end. The legs felt great, the hands were good. There might have been a few concessions to age; my reaction time wasn't quite as sharp, so I had to make a few adjustments. The last two years of my NHL career—one in Minnesota, the other in Hartford—weren't always easy. At the end it was difficult because I was a free agent without a contract. So I ended up signing one-year contracts…basically taking whatever I could. It was a humbling experience because during my prime I had played on either a first or second line. Now I was playing on a fourth line and getting limited ice time. Sometimes I was only getting five or six minutes per game.

Things got a little better that season with the Whalers after Pierre McGuire took over as head coach. I started getting more ice time. Even so, it was rather amazing that I did get those two aforementioned milestones. I knew I needed 29 points to get to four digits, and I wasn't playing that much. So I tried to make the best of the time afforded me. You learn to take advantage of the time you had. It was an odd season. There were rumors the Whalers were going to leave Hartford, which they did a couple years later when they moved to North Carolina.

The closing years were tough with all the injuries I endured. That made the decision to go to finish my career in France a lot easier. My shoulder just wasn't quite right and wouldn't hold up to the rigors of NHL play. Besides the ones I already listed, there had been the serious concussion—the result of the intent-to-injure hit by Chelios back in 1989. They all started adding up. Looking back, the decision to retire at that time was a smart move because I was still playing pretty well. As the old saying goes, better to get out a year too early than a year too late.

The funny thing is, I was playing less but making more money. Salaries started to jump up in the mid-'90s. If you hung on for a year or two, you were bound to make more money than you had in some years earlier in your career. But there was some guilt involved. I didn't want to just hang around and pick up a paycheck. If I really couldn't help a team or make a significant impact, it was time to say goodbye.

I was left wondering just how much longer I could have played if not for the injuries, which took a lot out of me.

One of the worst happened in 1985. We were playing the Buffalo Sabres, and I was cutting across the middle of the ice at the blue line when I collided with defenseman Lindy Ruff. I wasn't wearing a protective eye visor (they were not mandatory yet). Ruff went to make contact and inadvertently lifted my stick, which caught me squarely in the eye. Immediately I saw stars. It was pretty scary because it was similar to the injury our Hall of Fame goalie Bernie Parent suffered that ended his career. I had only been in the NHL for about six years and was just reaching the peak of my career. The last thing I needed was an injury to force an early retirement.

We didn't make that much money at the time, so if the injury had forced me to leave the game I probably would have struggled financially. Thankfully I only missed eight games. You can bet I quickly put on a visor. Nearly 40 years later, I still have some spots in my eye, possibly the result of the high fever I endured in the hospital post-injury. All in all, it was a scary experience.

A year later, I had more bad luck. I suffered a serious knee injury during a game against the Edmonton Oilers in Philadelphia at the old Spectrum. That year I was on pace to finish the season with well over 100 points. I did break the 90-point mark four times in my career but the eight games I missed left me just three points short of triple digits. To be honest, I was one of the best players on the team that year. If

I hadn't missed those games, I'm sure I definitely would have reached the 100-point milestone.

The rehab wasn't fun. I had to use this diabolical machine to flex my knee for a couple hours a day. They were trying to straighten the leg and build up the muscles. Trainer Pat Croce was working me out in an attempt to get me back as quickly as possible, yet it still took a couple weeks to get back to some semblance of full strength. The injury happened in December, and I was able to get rolling again with a few months still left in the season. By the time we got to the 1987 playoffs, I was actually a little fresher than I would have been if I had played every game. There was no lasting effect, which is why I was able to play as well as I did in the 1987 Stanley Cup Final and the Canada Cup.

You never really know how a knee is going to react. I still have some soreness in that knee from time to time. It was difficult to get through that, but I was still fairly young and didn't know much better.

Hockey can be a cruel game at times. In the back of your mind, you're always on the lookout for what could be a dangerous hit by someone with bad intentions. But sometimes an injury can happen in what seems like a safe play when it first develops. Failing to turn away from a hard but clean hit along the boards can have negative consequences.

Plus, the game is so fast, you often have to make split-second decisions. Let's say you're speeding into a corner to retrieve a puck and out of the corner of your eye you spot a 230-pound defenseman with the same intention. Do you pause for just an instant to avoid a potential catastrophic collision, or do you try to win this race and secretly breathe a sigh of relief when you manage to escape unscathed?

One thing I learned over the years is if you are a consistent scorer, especially in close, there's often going to be a target on your back. Other teams want to stop you by hook or by crook. Career-wise, I secretly wonder how many penalties I caused opponents to take...and how many the officials missed.

The toughest injury came, of course, in 1989 when Montreal defenseman Chris Chelios put that dirty hit on me during the Eastern Conference finals in the playoffs. I was leading the scoring in the playoffs prior to that. Chelios really knocked me out. But I only missed a game. It probably should have been a lot worse than that, and I'm not sure I should have even been playing, given the severity of the concussion. I did pass all the baseline tests to get into uniform, but I probably should have held off on that a bit.

It was really scary because I almost died. As I recovered, I wondered if I would ever feel the same again. Late in the series, our goaltender, Ron Hextall, went after Chelios and put a pretty good beating on him in Game 6. I really loved that because Hexy really stood up for me. I don't know if coach Paul Holmgren was exactly thrilled about it because he may have thought we still had a chance at the Stanley Cup Final, but I will always admire Ron for sticking up for me.

I was never the same after that concussion. I always knew that if I kept playing the same fearless way, I would have to make sure that I didn't feel like I was hurt. It was always in the back of my mind for the next couple years, and it affected how I played. I didn't want to go into the corners because I was scared to get hit again like that. I battled through it.

My faith made a big difference. Our team psychologist, Steve Rosenberg, made a couple of tapes for me to get me thinking positively again.

It's safe to say 1989 wasn't one of my luckier years. That same season, I sustained a significant hand injury in November. I found out I had a hole in the artery in my left hand. It's one of the toughest injuries in hockey because it affects everything you do—shooting, passing, defending. I wound up missing 27 games. The thought of retirement did cross my mind, but we weren't making that much money, so there was that to consider. I fought through it.

Then, after 11 years with the Flyers and the team on the way to a non-playoff season, general manager Bob Clarke did me that favor and traded me to the powerhouse Boston Bruins. I was going to be a free agent anyway, so there was really no use sticking around in Philadelphia. Plus, my former teammate and good friend Dave Poulin also wound up in Beantown, so there was that to look forward to. The Bruins were No. 1 in the Eastern Conference and would go on to play the powerhouse Oilers in the Cup Final.

When that season ended, I signed with the old Minnesota North Stars. A year later, my next injury was a right shoulder dislocation. I ended up playing only 51 games, plus one playoff game, which turned out to be my last. I tried to rehab it, but it's tough to do in-season. The joint keeps slipping out again. I had surgery at the end of the season.

With all the injuries, I was thinking, *This isn't getting any easier.* In fact, it was getting tougher every year. Missing all those games was starting to wear on me. The thing was, I was just starting to make more money, good money, but I needed some help to make it to the finish line. Fortunately, my old teammate, Paul Holmgren, was the general manager of the Whalers and he brought me in for one last go-round. I knew I was getting close to the end, so I just did my best.

When I finally decided to call it quits, I did so with a clear conscience. I had reached the milestones I wanted to achieve, played in five championship series, and earned some honor and respect for my career. I'm sure the folks back home were proud of me, and I knew the guys who played with me and against me knew I was one of the better players of my era. You can't ask for much more than that.

CHAPTER 19

PUTTING CELEBRITY
TO GOOD USE

JUST ABOUT EVERY NOTEWORTHY professional athlete, active or retired, gets the urge to give something back to the community that helped make them a celebrity. After all, without loyal fans there would be no games under bright lights in the big cities and beamed across countries on television and radio.

Although I had played hockey in several North American cities after my tenure with the Flyers, I knew that Philadelphia was going to be my final destination once the lights went low on my career. I had participated in my fair share of charity activities, such as golf tournaments, so I had a pretty good idea of what made a popular event work.

Perhaps the best and simplest way to generate funds came through golf tournaments. First, many (if not most) hockey players hit the little white ball around once the sticks-and-pucks season comes to an end. In fact, the time-worn joke is that, as soon as a team is eliminated, newspaper stories provide a little jab by reporting "they're headed for the golf course tomorrow!"

The Philadelphia area is blessed with some great golf courses, including (USA No. 1) Pine Valley, Merion, and Aronimink. Merion has hosted five U.S. Opens (1934, 1950, 1971, 1981, and

2013). It has tradition and some of the most picturesque scenery you could lay your eyes on. The second tier of establishments is equally impressive, which partly accounts for why the game is so popular in the Delaware Valley.

I started my own tournament at Blue Heron Pines in Galloway, New Jersey, while I was still playing in the NHL. It was toward the end of my playing career (1990 to 1994) and benefited the Make-A-Wish Foundation. This charity helps children (ages two to 18) who are suffering severe illnesses. It fulfills their wishes, such as giving a young boy dreaming of becoming a policeman someday the chance to spend a day with a police officer and get to know more about them and their line of work.

During the '90s, about 30 celebrity hockey players got involved, including Flyers Hall of Famer Bob Clarke, who was and is a legend in Philadelphia. Gene Hart, "the Voice of the Flyers," was a big help to us. Organizing the tournament was a good way for me and everyone else to give back. In the first four years of the tournament we raised close to $100,000 to make some wishes come true.

My brother-in-law, Bill McCay, is a professional photographer, and that helped with publicity and getting the word out about the tournament. One of the great things about Make-A-Wish is the relationships it formed. A lot of the players there hung out with the golfers who participated in the event. It really made me feel good because I felt like I was doing something for the people who had helped me along the way.

In the early 2000s, I was involved in the Calkins Media "Dollars for Citizen Scholars" tournament played at Jericho National Golf Club in New Hope. Once again, a number of Flyers alumni, including buddies such as Craig Berube and Keith Jones, helped out. Those two gentlemen helped keep the mood quite light.

More recently I started another tournament of my own at RiverWinds Golf Course in Deptford, New Jersey. Proceeds benefit the Stroke Center at the University of Pennsylvania. It goes without saying this is an organization that is near and dear to my heart because I am a survivor of just such a health threat. This particular facility is headed up by Dr. Scott Kasner, a neurologist at the University of Pennsylvania's Perelman Center.

We plan to have the tournament back in 2024. Former Eagles quarterback Ron Jaworski, who led the Birds to their 1981 Super Bowl appearance, has been helping me along the way.

While golf is a great venue to raise money for charity, hockey has its place as well. While working with Wolf Commercial Real Estate Company for nearly nine years, I put together four tournaments, which raised approximately $60,000 for each event, in the New Jersey area. I put the teams together with a mix of celebrity professionals blended in. Besides that, we did some work for the Multiple Sclerosis Research Institute. That event produced about another $30,000.

What impresses me most at a lot of these charity events is the generosity of fans, well-wishers, and volunteers who give so freely of their time as well as their donations. Many want to interact with their favorite sports star, but nearly all realize they are helping with a higher cause, namely assistance to those in need.

You can tell by the smiles on their faces that everyone is not only having a good time but feeling good about themselves. The conversations are lively, and the mood is upbeat. I believe it's a good thing for professional athletes to connect with their loyal followers and express appreciation for their support. I know in Philadelphia there's an emotional bond that goes beyond the arena of competition. When an athlete takes a moment to sign an autograph or jump into a photograph, it's more than just a token gesture. This goes on well after an athlete has retired, too.

That's what I enjoy most about signing a hat or shirt or smiling for a camera in a group shot. In a way, it's a form of payback. You want people to know that you realize how important their support is in the big picture. It's what makes the Philadelphia sports scene such a special place.

On April 1, 2023 (no joke, folks!), I organized another hockey event. This one was for the HEADstrong Foundation, a cancer nonprofit. My wife, Eileen, is on the board of the organization, so we raised money for that. A lot of the guys I played hockey with will be there. These guys know why they're here; it's about more than just playing hockey. It really helps a lot of people. The support so far has been truly amazing. I can't really describe how gratifying it is to give more of yourself than just writing a check and dropping it in the mail.

By the time the decade of the '90s was coming to an end and I had been out of the game for some five years, I was in a position to receive some recognition of my own. On a game night in 1999 I was inducted into the Flyers Hall of Fame. My teammate, Mark Howe, did the emcee honors and team owner Ed Snider stepped to the microphone, said some kind words, and talked about my famous "Guffaw" gesture. The fans went bonkers. It was a very special moment for me. I loved that the Flyers had put me in their Hall of Fame. It's an honor I don't take lightly.

That same year, an honor of perhaps equal prestige was bestowed upon me. The MasterCard All-Time Canadian Junior Hockey team was announced. The team included Bernie Parent in goal, Denis Potvin and Bobby Orr on defense, and Mario Lemieux (center) and Guy Lafleur (right wing) up front. The third forward at left wing? Me.

The announcement was made in Canada's capital, Ottawa, and it turned into a whole weekend of events. That supposedly was a conglomeration of the best six players in the history of Canadian Junior, and who could argue? No one could really challenge me at left wing because I held all the scoring records at that position.

There's no way to relate how that recognition made me feel. It meant a lot to me. And by the way, I'm the only one on that lineup who is not in the Hockey Hall of Fame.

Yet.

CHAPTER 20

BUILDING A GRASSROOTS HOME FOR HOCKEY

F INDING OUTDOOR WINTER ICE to skate on was never a problem for young players like me growing up in the '60s and early '70s in frigid Saskatchewan. This was long before the start of climate change, which has had a profound effect on thermometer readings in substantial parts of Canada and the United States. We just bundled up, sometimes as early as November, and headed for the nearest frozen lake. Trips to indoor rinks were only reserved for games and organized practices at the youth level.

Prior to the Flyers' arrival in 1967, there weren't a whole lot of indoor facilities to speak of in the greater Philadelphia metropolitan area. With the Flyers' success in the '70s, things began to change. Plus, outdoor ice was always a bit iffy, prone to sporadic gaps due to snowstorms or the occasional above-freezing temperatures during the winter months.

After my retirement from the NHL in the mid-'90s, I wanted hockey players—young and old—to have a place to play year-round right in my neck of the woods in South Jersey, just across the Delaware from the City of Brotherly Love. I chose the town of Medford, New Jersey, only about 10 miles from the Flyers' practice rink (Flyers Training Center) in Voorhees, New Jersey.

We started from scratch, and it took more than a year to build the rink. I thought I knew a lot about hockey rinks, but I certainly learned much more by going through the building process, with all the preparation, all the construction. Working with one of the owners, Len Fox, we put together a pro shop, a kitchen. It took quite a while to build it the right way.

This was another good experience for me. I got to meet a lot of people in the local community who were really enthusiastic about hockey and could truly appreciate another indoor facility. Without getting too technical, this was a sand-based rink (and there's plenty of that stuff in South Jersey). The refrigeration units were placed into the ground and the pipes were laid in such a way that you could watch them as they were put in order. The tricky part was hauling sand into that area by way of wheelbarrow. It took 10 days alone just to complete that task. It had to be done the right way. The sand had to be soaked to make sure it was level and didn't have bubbles.

The head of the project, Brian Lieg, did a really good job overseeing everything. Let me just say that the whole thing was not all that easy. A lot of the work with the sand base had to be done by hand. Later, all the boards had to be precisely laid in. We were doing everything to adhere to the original blueprint, right down to the big firewall (with sprinklers) in front to prevent a small problem getting out of hand. Later we added a skate rental room and a front counter to pay daily skating fees.

When it was finally completed, the large number of regular public skaters took us by surprise, but it showed how many people have an interest in this form of exercise and relaxation. From this I oversaw all the "how to play hockey" programs. We taught beginners how to skate. Then there were hockey camps in the summer, which included workout programs.

It was kind of neat because we had a lot of young kids, mostly between the ages of six and 12, and they were interested in the how to play hockey program. A lot of them honed their skills by taking part in public skating. The support we received was amazing. To this day, I think a lot of those family members remember me because I had a Russian sable hat, which I got on a trip in 1990 to Moscow with the Minnesota North Stars. We went over there for the Russian training camp. While I was there, my heart was set on buying one of those big hats. You can't really get those anywhere else. For one thing, it sure helped to keep me warm. But it was also special because it come from a place, Russia, not too many people from our side of the world go to visit. This was an honest-to-goodness souvenir. Back home, I would skate around the ice with that hat on. People really appreciated that, and I think the kids in particular got a kick out of it.

When the Medford Rink opened in '97, we started some adult hockey in the morning, from 7 to 8:30 AM on Wednesdays and Fridays. We had ex-NHL players, such as my old pal Ray Allison and Andre Faust. It was somewhat organized, with two goalies and referees. I'll admit it was a pretty good workout. To this day, we still have that morning skate, only now it's at the Flyers Skate Zone in Pennsauken. The competition is still high-spirited, but there's always time to share a few laughs during the scrimmages.

There was one incident in that first year that sticks in my memory to this very day. Allison and I were on opposing teams and at one point, my stick went up high and caught him right in the face. He started bleeding instantly, and I felt really bad. He hurried off the ice and needed stitches to close the wound. Although we were close friends, he was really upset about the whole thing, and I couldn't blame him. I probably would have been a little bent out of shape if the tables had been turned.

Ray's never forgotten that. He had to go to work that day and the whole thing was a rather painful, inconvenient situation. Fortunately, he's forgiven me for that momentary mishap. He lives now in Myrtle Beach, South Carolina, and we talk all the time on the phone. We're still good friends.

That last year with Brandon, playing alongside Brad McCrimmon and Ray, remains in sharp focus in my memory. Getting to the Memorial Cup final was special. Then, it was incredible that we were all selected in the 1979 NHL Draft just a few slots apart in the first round. I went to Philadelphia, Brad to Boston, and Ray to Hartford. In fact, he was the first player the Whalers ever selected after they came over from the old World Hockey Association and joined the National Hockey League.

Ray was later traded to Philadelphia, and he put together two very good seasons of 17 and 21 goals with the Flyers in 1981–82 and 1982–83. He was an outstanding all-purpose player. But then he suffered a broken ankle in a game and was never quite the same player after that. He did make a brief appearance in the 1985 Stanley Cup Final and was on the roster for the 1987 team that went to the Final, but that was pretty much the end of the line for him as far as the NHL was concerned. It's difficult to stay in hockey's best league when you're not quite at your physical best.

Following the years at Medford, I was hired to work for Aflac Insurance (2002–07). I was an agent for them, and it was a good experience. This was during the years I was working with Tim Saunders in the Flyers' radio broadcast booth as an analyst. Around the same time I earned my financial license, which was a challenging proposition. I had to study a lot—they weren't just handing these things out to anybody.

In 2007 I even took a stab at politics. I ran for general assembly in Burlington, New Jersey, with Diane Allen. There was a lot to learn here, as well. I spent a lot of time walking around, meeting people throughout Burlington County, and trying to get them to vote for me. We knew it was going to be an uphill battle because there are a lot more Democratic voters in that area. I didn't win, but it was a good experience. It was easy to run; I didn't have any shady areas on my résumé and believed I could have helped several causes if I had been elected.

Right around the time I got started at the Medford Ice Rink, I usually did "the Guffaw." After I scored a goal, I would take off my glove and extend my arm out straight. I got that one from comedian Howie Mandel. The story behind that is Howie did some shows in Atlantic City and I went down to the Jersey Shore to catch one of his shows. I liked what he did and got a real kick out of his routine. I tried to copy him with the Guffaw, which started in the '80s. I told all the kids that I was helping, "OK, here's the Guffaw." What it means is, have a hearty laugh, some enjoyment. I told the kids to let their teachers know that if you get an "A" for a grade on a subject, then do a Guffaw (to celebrate).

A lot of the young kids found out about it, and some emulated it. I think for some, it's still a pretty big deal to this day. It brings a smile to my face just thinking about it.

CHAPTER 21

RADIO-ACTIVE FOR A DECADE

LOTS OF FLYERS FANS recall the night of May 4–5, 2000, because that's when the team played the longest game in team history—and came out on top.

For me, the difference was, I wasn't sitting in a comfortable chair at home watching on television. I was in Pittsburgh, sitting in the radio broadcast booth of the old Civic "Igloo" Arena, listening to the Penguins and Flyers go at it for the better part of seven hours.

Play-by-play man Tim Saunders was alongside me and calling this Stanley Cup playoff game was both fun and emotionally demanding. When the clock struck midnight, there was still more than two hours of hockey to be played.

As the night progressed, things got pretty weird. Despite the exciting nature of the game, people were falling asleep in the stands, only to be jarred awake when a hard shot barely missed the net. The scene was rather bizarre, to say the least.

Concession stands started running out of certain food and beverages. Later I learned that players were drinking that old favorite, Pedialyte (a concoction served to children that helps supply electrolytes), during intermissions. The Flyers' locker room floor was littered with empty pizza boxes and the remnants of whatever bits of nourishment the players could get their hands on.

Coaches on both teams told their players to take shorter shifts because the fatigue factor was beginning to exact its toll. By the third overtime, it was the equivalent of playing a "doubleheader." Flyers head coach Craig Ramsay had enjoyed a long career in the NHL and was known for his strong two-way play. This was crucial in the sudden-death situation because one slip-up and the game (and maybe the series) would be over. Ramsay was constantly looking up and down the bench to see which players might still have something left. It's safe to say nobody was raising their hand to volunteer for more playing time.

Pittsburgh had won the first two games of the best-of-seven series back in Philadelphia, so for the Flyers it was imperative to come away from the Steel City with at least one win. After regulation time ended, the two teams battled to a standoff for what amounted to nearly two more games. Finally, the Flyers' Keith Primeau started a rush, worked his way past Pittsburgh defenseman Darius Kasparaitis, and buried a high shot for the game-winner sometime well after 2 AM.

During the overtimes I had visited with some writers and done interviews in between periods. But pretty soon we were running out of writers to talk with and things to talk about. We had gone through most of the Philadelphia scribes. At least it was nice to be on the winning side. It's something I will remember for a long time, having played games in Pittsburgh and knowing how intense the rivalry was.

This was my first season on the radio, several years after my professional hockey career—much of it with the Flyers—had come to an end. I had been working on creating the aforementioned ice rink in Medford, New Jersey.

I started out halfway through the 1999–2000 season because Steve Coates was going to begin with television and chief operating officer Ron Ryan decided to make the change halfway through the season. Not exactly the ideal situation for someone like me who was just breaking into the business.

So they came to me without a whole lot of warning and offered me the radio analyst job. I only had a few days to make up my mind. At that point, I was pretty involved with the Medford rink. Things on the radio started out OK. Tim is a great guy to work with. He kept the mood light and didn't put me on the spot.

To be honest, I was really bad at the start. There were things I wanted to say, but it wasn't always easy putting them into words. So I had a couple of the team's television veterans, Gene Hart and Bill Clement, help me out the first two years. They gave me a lot of hints to get better. After every game, I would watch complete replays so I could tell what I needed to do to improve. On the radio, the analyst has to chime in as the play dictates and paint a picture of what's going on . . . then give it back to Saunders in a timely fashion to continue the play-by-play.

It took me a couple years to really get the hang of it. I was always learning new things and getting help from others. One thing I made sure of was to not keep saying the same things over and over again. And all the time I was looking for hints to get better. People were doing their best to give me feedback.

Travel to away games was always a lot of fun. We flew on charter planes or trains all the time. It wasn't always that way when I started to play, back in 1979. The broadcasters would sit in the back of the plane. There was a lot of card-playing or listening to music on portable players and headphones. Some were looking at magazines to scout the latest new cars.

Of course, I had a pretty good rapport with the players. I had only been retired for a few years, so most of them knew who I was. I talked with them a lot and even though I had been in the NHL for quite awhile, it was still pretty amazing chatting with active players.

Even though I was well respected as a retired player, that still didn't spare me from the "rookie" hazing ritual. Back when I was a first-year player in 1979–80, I had received a couple of "buzz" haircuts to make light of the fact I didn't deserve a whole lot of respect just yet. And so it was on a charter after one game when I made the mistake of falling asleep on the trip home. To put it mildly, there are times when I can be a very heavy sleeper and it might take a fire alarm to get me out of my slumber. When I finally woke up, to my surprise, half my tie was missing! Someone had found a pair of scissors and done the honors. It made for some good laughs all around. It wasn't too bad. I can't remember if someone replaced the tie.

There were plenty of good memories from my radio career, but one of the longest lasting involved trips to Madison Square Garden for Flyers–Rangers games. The place is billed as "The World's Most Famous Arena" and they're probably right. The fans are passionate but, more noteworthy for broadcasters, the sight lines are excellent. We were seated in the first level. So it was more exciting to be a part of everything. You were really close enough to appreciate the speed of the game.

In most NHL arenas, they had the radio guys stuck way up high so you couldn't feel like you were near the action and could follow the flow of the game really closely. But MSG was much better. I also had a fondness for Montreal because, even though you sat way up, the press box was in a "gondola" configuration, so you were looking down directly over the action. Therefore you were able to see all the plays developing.

Tim and I got along really well. He would make a lot of jokes and I would just play along. When I had the chance, I would add my two cents and make it a little more fun. As time went by, I think I loosened up a bit and really did a better job of describing how plays went and how they were going to go. I was always thinking about painting the right picture—quite important on a radio broadcast—and keeping in mind the people that were listening. It was a lot of fun and the feedback just kept getting better. Maybe that's why I stayed with it for the better part of a decade.

CHAPTER 22

LIGHTING IT UP

I MAY HAVE GROWN UP in a small town in the Canadian province of Saskatchewan, but in the years that I matured into an adult, I kept my eyes and ears open. I was open to trying new things. I watched to see how grown men (and women) found ways to relax.

We all know that smoking tobacco in large quantities on a regular basis is not good for one's health. But the occasional stogie, especially one to celebrate a special event, probably isn't a terrible thing.

Around 2018, I got the idea to create my own cigar brand. Cigars have been lit for hundreds of years and some even look at the whole thing as a sort of status symbol. And the higher quality the cigar, the better. Just like with my professional hockey career, if I was in for a dime, I was in for a dollar. I didn't want to associate my name with a substandard product.

Finding a name for the product was easy. Once I had adopted the "Guffaw" gesture, putting that tag on the cigar seemed natural. So I went with ex–Philadelphia Eagle Ken Dunek and my son, Jackson, to the Dominican Republic—a place, much like Cuba, known mainly for its cigars. Dunek, my son, and several other friends headed down to the DR for a five-day trip. We checked out a couple factories that produced cigars in the area. It was an educational experience. We learned how the cigars were cut, aged, and produced to a high standard.

I didn't smoke that much during my professional hockey career, but when I did it was always one of Cuba's finest. Of course they were expensive. When we set out to make our own cigars, we used those Cuban cigars as sort of the standard. The cheap ones, you noticed a big difference. They were loaded with filler. Ours were full-leaf. There are three types of cigars: mild, medium, and full-bodied.

The trip was fantastic. We played some fine golf courses, hit the best restaurants, and enjoyed some of the nightlife. It was then that I decided to make my own Guffaw Cigars. The name suggested noise, excitement, celebration. When I scored a goal, I did the Guffaw, I wanted something a little different. The fans picked up on that.

It took about a year to get everything ready. I worked with another company called Vivonté Cigars and a gentleman by the name of Glen Hamilton. Glen worked in the water segment of the energy sector for eight years and maintained a presence in the industry. His company Evolution Developments Corp. is active in renewable energy consulting as well as water filtration system solutions. He has been actively involved in developing utility and private sector renewable energy business in selected global markets.

Hamilton grew up in Hamilton, Saskatchewan, but he's been in the Dominican Republic for 25 years. He helped me create the blend. The idea was to initially create 425 cigars to commemorate my 425 National Hockey League goals. The cigars sold pretty well the first year. After one year, I said to myself, "OK, people love what we're doing." They appreciated the good blend and the fact that they smoked really well. At that point I figured that people would keep reordering.

Fairly soon I extended the length of the cigars from five inches to six inches. We made sure the price was not too expensive. The brand now sponsors several golf tournaments, including the Flyers Alumni annual event. We also are involved in several charity tournaments. People can buy them right there or online. Let me make this clear—it's not about making money. It's more the fun of creating something and identifying with the product. As long as the quality is good and people are happy, then so are we. Personally, I had to stop drinking alcohol after my stroke, so it was sort of compensation as a way to relax. No more beer or harder stuff for me. Just water and a good cigar.

After a decade of working in the radio broadcast booth at Flyers games, it was time to find a new challenge. The business world was always something that caught my imagination. Putting qualified people in the right career positions seemed like a great line of work. So that's how things got started when I joined the Judge Group in 2009.

Calling Flyers games with Tim Saunders had been a lot of fun, and the job allowed me to stay close to hockey and players I had either competed with or against. Still, setting off on my own at this particular time and place seemed like the right thing to do.

I wanted to start off in the business world in a field where the company helped people. And I wanted to get to know clients on a one-to-one, personal basis. I figured that's the most honest and open way to go about this sort of service.

Marty Judge ran the show along with Steve Donia, who's been there for almost 30 years. Marty's a great guy. He grew up in Philadelphia. He started his company quite a while back and now it's one of the best. His sense of humor might have something to do with that—it's second to none. When it comes to a party, he's often the life of it. But at the same time his work ethic could be called world class. It seems like everyone in this company works hard and some of that might have to do with the example Marty sets.

My relationship started with Judge because he's familiar with a lot of professional athletes, like former Eagles quarterback Ron Jaworski. As for me, having played for the Flyers helped me get my foot in the door. So there was a challenge right off the bat: the Judge offices were in Conshohocken, Pennsylvania, a western suburb of Philadelphia, while I was way over back east in New Jersey. Anyone who lives in the City of Brotherly Love can tell you trying to buck early morning traffic through crosstown roads is no bed of roses. Let's put it this way: you have lots of time to listen to the radio and let your mind wander when you're pretty much not moving.

So the best solution for the commute was to get up early—and I mean really early. I wound up rolling out of the sack at 5 AM and was on the road by 6. There's nothing quite like driving to work in the dark! But at least you beat all the traffic. Same deal in the afternoon. I would wait until everything cleared out and then head home around 7 PM. Not ideal, but better than pulling up stakes and moving. Plus, it gave me more time to get to know the business. I worked a lot and I loved it. And when you love your line of work, there's no clock-watching.

After a couple years, I was able to move downtown to the Judge Group office in Center City. This shortened the drive from and to home considerably. I could put my time to better use.

During my six years at Judge, I had a chance to meet quite a few of the top civic and business leaders in and around Philadelphia. A lot of them were CIOs and CEOs of companies based in the area. I wound up running four divisions for the Judge Group. They had quite a bit of staffing for IT medical services for Epic, for Delaware Valley hospitals. Also, they are involved with project work.

I really enjoyed this type of work. The nice thing about it was the company really looked after its people. Every six months the employees were invited to take trips. A lot of the personnel hailed from places like Mexico and Aruba. About 30 people would go on these five- or six-day getaways. This was a great way to meet all the other people working at the Judge Group.

Recently, the Judge Group has really expanded, with about 20 office sites throughout the world, including one in China. I was able to help them set up a couple golf events with customers. For what it's worth, we used my name to help open some doors. That helped secure some celebrity golfers to join in and help improve the numbers.

One of the big meeting places was the famous Union League in downtown Philadelphia, where we got to meet a lot of the local business leaders. The whole experience was a great way to transition from Flyers radio into what you might call the business world. The next step would be moving into the world of real estate with the Wolf Company.

When I was playing professional hockey, I wasn't thinking about post-career ambitions, although a lot of different ideas crossed my mind. I wanted something that would be challenging and get me involved with high-achieving people. Working with the Judge Group got me started, and then came an offer in commercial real estate.

I earned my broker's license in January 2015. I took the test, passed it, and went right to work for Jason Wolf at Wolf Commercial Real Estate. At the start we only had eight people working in the main office. From the very start, we were interested in building a great team filled with qualified people.

Almost all the business is commercial real estate. That includes leasing, buying properties, investing, and other things. I started working and getting in touch with some people that I knew.

But everything came to a grinding stop on September 3 of that year when I suffered the stroke. It was so nice of Jason Wolf to pay me for a year and a half as I recovered. That really made a big difference for me because I wasn't making that much money at the time. Every little bit helped.

So to this day I'm really thankful for what the company provided me and my family. I still work with Jason. It's going on eight years since I joined Wolf CRE and I have never regretted a day of it. We've done a lot of things together over eight-plus years. We've built a team to 20 people and they're excellent at what they do. Our name is well recognized in the area, but we can work all over the U.S. because we've partnered with CORFAC, which has 75 offices throughout the country. We have good connections there to work wherever we want.

Last year my wife, Eileen, put together a franchise called Prime IV Hydration & Wellness in Marlton, which opened in November 2023. Working with the right people and doing a good job really makes a big difference.

When I first got started, I set up a couple celebrity hockey events for Wolf. At this point, we've had four charity hockey events. We put together two teams, three lines, six defense, two goalies. Also, we made sure each team had six Flyers alumni members. That way everybody gets to play with a celebrity on the ice at the Flyers Training Center in Voorhees, New Jersey.

The events have raised a lot of money for charities. In 2022, about $80,000 was generated from the hockey event and another $60,000 came from the golf tournament. After the hockey games, the alumni stick around to talk with people, and of course that's one of the more popular sides of the activity. Plus there's a dinner put together in nearby Berlin, New Jersey. Lots of people have helped out, including longtime Flyers announcer Lou Nolan and former NHL referee Kerry Fraser.

The golf tournament has been close to my heart as well. Lots of linksters have shown up at Ramblewood Country Club in Mount Laurel, New Jersey. It's an annual event that sells out well in advance. Most of the money raised goes to the six charity organizations we support in the Philadelphia area.

Locally, in the commercial real estate business, everybody knows us. It's been a lot of fun. I enjoy working with Jason and his team. When you establish relationships in the community, the trust factor becomes second nature, so what more could you ask for?

Radio work might sound glamorous, but when it comes to the old paycheck, it's not quite what you might expect. At least not when I was serving as an analyst on Flyers broadcasts in the early 2000s. So that meant looking for some supplemental income. My first serious endeavor was securing a health license from Aflac.

A lot of the things that I did after I retired in 1995 put me on path to study a lot and take tests. I'll be honest: it was difficult. Unless you're familiar with the subjects, you're really starting from scratch. You don't know any better. I wanted to succeed at these kinds of things because I played pro hockey in the era just before salaries in the sport exploded.

My license with Aflac spanned the years from 2002 to 2007. My position had me selling insurance to those who seemingly needed it. A lot of people are aware of the Aflac brand, maybe because of the TV commercials with the white duck who can speak basically one word: "AFLAC!" Doing this required keeping up with all the rules and guidelines—you're tested every year or so to make sure you're still on top of it.

Once the license ran out, I moved over to HarborLight Investment. Well, the medical license might have been challenging but obtaining a financial license was even tougher. I obtained my Series 6, which means that you had passed a lot of tests and learned a lot, which was difficult. But I made it through and became the proud holder of the aforementioned license. One of the perks of the job was one of the offices was in Manasquan, a town down at the Jersey Shore. While it was a fairly long commute from my home in western New Jersey, I really didn't mind. I knew so many people and it was gratifying to be able to help them with their financial situation.

The best part of all this was it kept me active when I wasn't working with the Flyers. You learn a lot of stuff along the way, and it challenges you mentally to do other things besides talk about hockey.

CHAPTER 23

"JUST KEEP UP
YOUR HOPE"

ONE OF THE GREATEST THINGS a disabled person can do is help others who are in a similar medical situation. In other words, the best enablers are those who have been through the experience and learned about the best ways to get better.

This is why I decided to join the Bancroft organization in 2019 and was with them until 2022. Bancroft is a leading regional nonprofit that provides services for individuals with autism and intellectual and developmental disabilities, as well as neurological rehabilitation.

Toni Pergolin, the CEO, met with me, and I signed a contract with them for three years. I really loved it. They have an office in Mount Laurel, New Jersey, where the brain and stroke treatment personnel are. Some patients visit every day. I was there on an intermittent basis. At the start, I did some occupational and physical therapy just for rehabilitation of the fingers on my right hand, which were affected by the stroke in 2015. We did stretching and balance exercises just to feel better, and I can say that it made a big difference working with them. The people there are great to work with, and I developed a great affection for them. They make it a very enjoyable experience.

When I joined they were conducting monthly meetings. I started off by doing some videos for them, which were posted on their website, along with a presence on Instagram, Facebook, and other social media outlets. The videos included information about different events in which I was going to be participating. Soon after, Bancroft published some information cards so that every person I met received a signed card from Bancroft along with a personal note to say "Just keep up your hope," because a lot of those people in wheelchairs have medical conditions much worse than I do. Thankfully for me, the affected areas are limited to the fingers on my right hand and some issues with the right side of my body.

I'm still disabled, and I have to remember that. I can tell you this: the brain takes a lot of time to heal. So you have to make sure that you keep doing things that can help you get better. I think being proactive and talking with people about strokes and brain injuries really helps me.

I still have aphasia, which means that words don't always come out the way you intended. But I've come a long way from that. When I slow my speech down a bit, it usually works better. Every three months or so I delivered speeches for Bancroft to a bunch of people in a room, talking about my stroke and how I recovered—how people need to have help to get better. I also stressed that affected people needed to take their time, have faith—don't give up, and keep up your rehab because after the initial participation, people don't do rehab as much. And so I tell people to keep up with that rehab because it does make a difference.

The message is certainly getting out there. Bancroft holds big events at the casinos in Atlantic City. They also have events with other rehab facilities in the Delaware Valley. I was usually in attendance at those events. I would meet with other people just to get the Bancroft name out. There's also a golf event at Galloway National Golf Club down at the Jersey Shore. Of course I was a part of that. We would set up on a short par-3, hit some shots, take some photographs, and exchange ideas through conversations with people. Bancroft is a 501(c)(3) nonprofit, so it was encouraging to help it raise money through events like this. Another fun event is a run/walk 5K along with other activities near their South Jersey headquarters, which has facilities for overnight stays, including a gymnasium, a kitchen, a swimming pool, the whole works.

For me, it was great just to meet the people under Bancroft's care to learn about their problems. I had a chance to converse with them and exchange ideas and experiences. In fact, I've kept a list of people who have brain injuries or are stroke victims who I try to keep up with and give hope and encouragement. If they need some other help, I try to assist there, too.

I have to remember that I'm very fortunate to be in pretty good shape and probably better off than others. I know for me it would have been tough if I didn't have balance or my legs didn't work right. If I had been left with an inability to skate or play golf, it would have been a lot tougher for me to get better. I keep that in mind all the time.

It's not always easy to train the brain in certain athletic situations when you're on the comeback trail. In some respects, it's all about accepting new limitations. It's sort of how things go as one grows older. As the years go by, those 280-yard golf drives become 250, then maybe 220, and so on. The difference for a stroke survivor is the process doesn't take years; it happens almost overnight. You go out to the golf course, walk up to that first tee, and, although you've braced yourself for this new world, it still takes some getting used to.

That said, the challenge is almost the same as when you picked up the game as a youth. Only now, you see the game from a different perspective. However, a good shot in these new circumstances can be just as rewarding as it would have been before.

Encouragement from others also helps. In the past, "good shot" might have translated simply to "way to go." Now, the underlying message is, "Good shot, and that's pretty impressive for a guy who's been through what you've been."

Bancroft put a video together of me after a year and a half getting better. In 2019, that video won an international award. A lot of the video focused on conversations I had with people at the Hollydell Ice Arena in Sewell, New Jersey, and included images of me getting back on skates and moving around the ice for the first time after my stroke. They did a really nice job with that, and I felt like the award was justified.

I'll never forget that first time back on the ice. It just felt so good because that's what I loved doing. Even though my hand doesn't work, and I can't shoot the puck that much, I can still skate OK. The video reminds me every time I skate how fortunate I am and how lucky I am to be a part of all the things that are going on.

Through Bancroft, I met some people who keep doing golf tournaments, and I'm always there to help. There's an annual gala event that was interrupted due to the Covid-19 pandemic, but it's still raised something like $600,000 and nearly all the money goes back into patient care. It goes a long way toward the people who need the help.

CHAPTER 24

DECK THE HALLS

I'M NOT THE TYPE WHO lives for awards, but I appreciate it when my NHL career gets recognized for its merit. For instance, in January 2014, I was inducted into the All Sports Museum in southern New Jersey. It was a small accolade, but it was nice to be honored for what I had achieved. It was a chance to get some friends together, along with family members, and that was probably the most gratifying part of the event.

Perhaps the most significant honor was my induction into the Saskatchewan Hockey Hall of Fame, also in 2014. The ceremony was held in Prince Albert, which is not far from the province capital of Saskatoon. Everyone was there, including my mom and dad and brothers and sisters. It was a really nice event. There had to be close to 500 people in attendance, and several other standouts from the province were honored as well. It was really special for me that my family was there and able to be part of that. That was the same year the late, great Brad McCrimmon was also inducted. We had come up through the junior ranks at the same time and later been teammates on the Flyers. He had died in the plane crash in Russia. To accept the honor were his widow, Maureen, along with the couple's children, son Liam and daughter Carlin.

It's so nice to be recognized for all the hockey you've been playing for years. I was very thankful that my dad, a Lutheran minister, could attend because I knew he was proud of me. He taught me to be humble and to give back.

One position I'm particularly proud of is serving on the Flyers' Alumni Board, something I've done since 2014. I help them with all the events they have. It's special for me because I did the radio for nine years, I played for 15 years (11 with the Flyers), and I was an ambassador for every home game from 2016 to 2020.

My induction into the Philadelphia Sports Hall of Fame also came in 2014. I was inducted along with longtime New York Rangers goaltender Mike Richter, who hails from the Philadelphia suburb of Flourtown. A lot of the Flyers Alumni were part of that. It was quite a milestone in my career because a lot of great athletes have competed in Philadelphia sports.

And now to the one thing missing in my trophy case: the Hockey Hall of Fame. I think my credentials speak for themselves. More than a thousand points, more than a thousand games, and five trips to the Stanley Cup Final with three different teams. Oh, well; maybe someday…

I did receive a great "consolation" prize in 1999: induction into the Flyers Hall of Fame. There are some pretty impressive names on that list: Clarke, Barber, Parent, Lindros, Howe—not to mention the gentlemen off the ice who meant so much to the Flyers, such as Ed Snider, Fred Shero, Keith Allen, and Gene Hart.

To see my name up in the rafters every time I visit the Wells Fargo Center means a lot. Many of the other names up there played in my era. Two of the most recent—Rick Tocchet and Paul Holmgren—were instrumental in my career. Rick was a heart-and-soul player who would do whatever it took to win, be it a big goal, a hard hit, a fight, or a fiery locker room speech. Paul was my coach with two different NHL teams and always had my best interests in mind.

Most of the best moments of my career took place in Philadelphia, and so I'm grateful that enough people thought enough of me to have my name positioned with most of the other greats to have played in that city.

I've given away most of my trophies to my family members. I don't really care about awards. What am I going to do with them? The actual trophies and plaques don't mean that much to me. Having gone through so many injuries, I'm just grateful my hockey career lasted as long as it did. I'm thankful I've been able to help people and if I'm recognized for that, so be it.

CHAPTER 25

FAVORITE MEMORIES

I DON'T NEED TO HAVE TOO MUCH inner debate about which are my favorite hockey memories because there are almost too many to count. Whether it was in the days of my youth, my prime years in the National Hockey League, or even a couple alumni games, I usually seemed to be in the right place at the right time to make a difference. The kick for me was always about helping my team, and that was fairly evident, because I played some of my best hockey on the road to the Stanley Cup Final with three different teams.

In my growing years, the scoring numbers were a bit ridiculous because there wasn't a whole lot of emphasis placed on defense. It was pretty much just end-to-end action with not a lot of slowing down. In one game when I was 13, I scored a rather amazing 15 goals. That's usually about a season's worth for some players. If nothing else, it sort of served notice that I was going to be a go-to guy, even when the competition started getting tougher.

At age 16 there was a game where everything seemed to click. I scored five goals in a game for the Melville Millionaires. It seemed like every time I shot, the puck had a chance to go in. A year later, I turned on the red light seven times for Brandon in a game against Portland. That's a Western Hockey League record that still stands to this day. In those days, players didn't get drafted until they were age 20 (the qualifying age now is 18), so I was still in the junior ranks at 19. That year, I finished the season with 94 goals. Yes, you read that right—94. Sounds like something Wayne Gretzky or Mario Lemieux might do. The last goal came against my brother Ron's team, Regina.

That same season, I produced a record-setting 16 game-winning goals, which also remains a record in the WHL.

My rookie season, the good times kept rolling. In the fall of 1979, I joined the Flyers as a rookie, but my confidence was still quite high. Hockey history books will show the LCB line of Reggie Leach, Bob Clarke, and Bill Barber was, for a few years, one of the most successful in NHL history, but I also had a chance to play with Clarke and Leach. I was actually on their line when I scored my first goal against New York Islanders goalie Billy Smith, who would go on to win four Stanley Cups. The goal ended up being the game-winner. What a thrill! I had an assist in that game as well, and that's a night I will never forget.

Soon after we embarked on that professional sports record 35-game unbeaten streak (25–0–10). I registered a point in 25 of those games. Not bad for a first-year guy. Later that year, when we played in the Stanley Cup Final against those pesky Islanders, I had three goals in six games, but we lost in a Game 6 overtime fare-thee-well. There's not a player from that Flyers team who didn't think we would have won the Cup if we somehow had dragged that series back to Philadelphia and the raucous Spectrum for a decisive Game 7. In the ultimate tiebreaker, Bob Nystrom scored off a two-on-one and that was that.

One of the most memorable goals of my career came in the 1982 World Championships in Finland. The Soviet Union won the title, but they had a tough time beating Canada, which still had a lot of players involved in the Stanley Cup playoffs. The final score was Soviet Union 4, Canada 3, and one of those goals for

Canada was scored by me against one of the best goaltenders in history, Vladislav Tretiak. That was a special goal for me.

Another one for the books came in Game 6 of the 1987 Stanley Cup Final against Gretzky and the Edmonton Oilers. Edmonton raced to a 3–1 lead in the best-of-seven series but somehow we won Game 5 up in Alberta and staved off elimination. I had four assists in that game, and it was probably the best performance I've ever put on as we won 4–3. Then we came back to Philadelphia to a packed house at the Spectrum for Game 6. The Oilers were leading as the two teams headed late into the third period when I scored with about six minutes left to tie the score 2–2. The Spectrum was really loud. It was bedlam. Just when you thought it couldn't get any louder, J.J. Daigneault scored the game-winner a few minutes later, and you couldn't hear yourself think. Some veteran fans said it was the loudest they ever heard the Spectrum, before or after.

In Game 7, we led early on a goal by Murray Craven. It was a power-play goal. Our confidence was high. Then I had a shot that appeared to be going into the net. But defenseman Charlie Huddy, backing up goaltender Grant Fuhr, somehow managed to get a piece of it with his stick. If the puck had gone in, it would have made the score 2–0, and who knows where it would have gone after that? We might have won the Stanley Cup that year.

It seemed like the Flyers were always running into some dynasty during their post–Stanley Cup years, in which they reached the Cup Final four times in 11 seasons. I was on three of those Flyers teams. Prior to my arrival, the Flyers were denied the chance to make it three straight Stanley Cups in 1976 as a budding Montreal Canadien regime was just getting started. Without injured goaltender Bernie Parent, the Flyers never had a chance. The Habs won in four straight and went on to win the next three Stanley Cups as well.

In 1980, it was the same story, different opponent. The Islanders had been contenders throughout the late '70s and finally put it together in '80. Their first victims? The Flyers. The Isles would go on to win three more Cups in that four-year run.

And then came the Oilers powerhouse, winning five Cups between 1984 and 1990. I was on the wrong end of three of those titles.

After I retired, the Flyers made the Stanley Cup Final again in 1997 but lost to Detroit in four straight. The Red Wings would win again in 1998, 2002, and 2008. Last but not least, the Flyers fell to the Chicago Blackhawks in the ultimate round in 2010. Chicago would win two more Cups in the next few years.

Do you see a pattern there?

In, 1990, I was playing for the Boston Bruins after the trade from the Flyers. I played in the NHL All-Star Game on a line with Lemieux and Boston's Cam Neely. Mario had four goals and he won the MVP and with it, a fancy new car. My finest moment came when I completed a checking assignment on Gretzky and held him without a point. Who knew I was a Selke Trophy candidate? I backchecked like the dickens, and he didn't even get a point.

Later that season the Bruins reached the Stanley Cup Final against—who else?—the Oilers. The first game was in Boston and, wouldn't you know it, the lights went out for about 25 minutes. You could almost hear the muscles tightening up in the locker rooms. It figured that the delay wasn't enough adversity, now the game went into overtime. I'll always remember that defenseman Glen Wesley of the Bruins had an empty net to score but he somehow missed it. If we had won that first game, it might have given us some momentum. But it wasn't to be. In the third overtime, Edmonton's Petr Klíma scored to win it for the Oilers. From there, Edmonton dominated the series (without Gretzky, who had been traded to Los Angeles back in 1988) and went on to win its fifth Stanley Cup in seven years.

The next year, I was in a Minnesota uniform, and in Game 1 of the opening series against the Chicago Blackhawks, I scored the game-winner in overtime and we were on our way. Somehow the North Stars made it all the way to the Cup Final against Mario and the Penguins. This was my third final in five years with three different teams. Go figure. The Penguins won the championship, but it was a great experience for me.

Three years later, now with the Whalers, I was wrapping up my NHL career when I was on the verge of registering my 1,000th point. The opponent? My old pals, the Philadelphia Flyers. The game was at the Spectrum, and I scored two goals. A lot of fans cheered, and I appreciated that. Chris Pronger had one of the assists. You couldn't have scripted it any better. That was a big milestone for me. Just before that, I was in Los Angeles for a game against the Kings. It was my 1,000th game and Gretzky was on the ice to make the occasion that much more meaningful.

While my professional playing days were over, I hadn't lost my love for hockey. So we started a men's league at the rink we built in Medford, New Jersey. Today we still play at the Skate Zone in Pennsauken, New Jersey. I really look forward to that, especially after my stroke. It took a few years after that to feel well enough to play again. I love playing hockey, even though it's low-key, because it means so much to me.

Another highlight from my "golden years" came in 2012, when we played a game as part of the Flyers–New York Rangers outdoor extravaganza in Philadelphia. There were a lot of players on both alumni squads, so my ice time was limited. But I got to play with former teammates Dave Poulin and Tim Kerr.

CHAPTER 26

STARTING OVER

B Y THE EVENING OF September 3, 2015, I was alert enough to know my life had changed forever. Lying in a hospital bed and contemplating what had just happened, I could still think with enough clarity to know I had just suffered a major stroke. I couldn't talk, I couldn't walk, and I didn't even know if things would get worse before they got better. All I could do was believe and have faith that eventually my health would improve and I could get back to some semblance of normal.

Those first hours were some of the darkest. When you don't know if you will even be around to see tomorrow, it can be humbling.

All my life up to that point I was able to accomplish pretty much everything I wanted to do from a physical standpoint. I was fortunate enough to be blessed with the tools to perform in a sport like hockey at the highest level. Now, almost in the blink of an eye, a significant portion of that natural-born skill was gone.

I was really determined to find it again, but something inside me told me it wasn't going to be easy or fast. There were going to be a lot of hurdles and persistence was going to be the only way to make it through. Giving up or giving in just isn't in my nature. If there was a way to find a path back to a somewhat normal existence, I was going to exhaust just about every possibility. I didn't care how many hours it took or how many dollars it was going to cost, I was on a mission to reclaim my life.

Truth be told, I had lots of time in a hospital bed to contemplate what I had just gone through, where I was at, and where I intended to get back to.

It was really frustrating, but my faith made a big difference because my father was a Lutheran minister, and I had the support of my entire family. Later, I had a chance to visit some of my friends, including Scott McKay and Ray Allison. They stopped by just to see how things were going. The Flyers Alumni did a really great job of supporting me, as did some of the people I stayed friends with back in Canada and those I play hockey with in New Jersey.

The stroke came from out of the blue. One minute I was sound asleep, the next I was still out of it but tumbling over the side of the rental house bed. My face hit the side of the bed and suddenly my faculties were gone. I didn't know what was going on. I was pretty much out of it. They got me to the hospital pretty quickly. It was really scary, because every time I tried to speak or move, very little happened. I didn't know what was going on. At the time I was with my wife, Kris, my daughter, Paige, and my son, Jackson. All I could do was point to everything. The frustration level was high.

Initially, there wasn't much I could do. I just stayed in the bed, watched television, and did what I could to communicate. After five days, from there I was transferred to Magee Rehabilitation Center in Philadelphia. For six weeks, I took a needle in the stomach every day to control what was going on. I still had those three hours of speech therapy every day. They still had to move me around in a wheelchair just to take a test or something of that nature.

The uncertainty was the hardest part. No one knew for sure if I would ever be able to talk or walk again. So many of these functions we take for granted until they're taken away from us. The frustration level was beyond belief. Finally there was some relief. I was able to pull myself up and out of the wheelchair and take a few steps. Talk about starting all over again—balance, for a healthy person, is usually on autopilot. But here, it was take each step very carefully so as not to slip and fall. It felt good to be upright.

You have already read about how impatient I was to do more. So you can imagine what it was like to be around me after a month of basic confinement to my sleeping quarters. I got the green light to walk out of my room, and it was like a jailbreak! I was able to make it down to the dining area. This was great not only for the food, but also the chance to talk with other people more on a face-to-face level.

At this point, three hours of speech therapy didn't seem all that daunting. In fact, I thought I was capable of doing more. It should come as no surprise I was always looking for something to do. I was given the OK to water the plants in my room and take care of them. The chore of cleaning up the room was a welcome addition to the daily schedule and, again, the semblance of getting "back to normal."

A few words about repairing my speech—it probably took longer than I expected. I couldn't really communicate at first. I would just point. But I wanted that to get better because you want the person to know exactly what you're thinking, which can only come about through verbalizing the desired thought. Gradually my reflexes started to improve. The occupational therapy really helped. Since my feet weren't really affected by what happened, that at least gave me a steady platform when it came to getting more ambulatory.

One of the challenging parts of this physical recovery was the damage that was done to the nerves in the fingers of my right hand. Basically they partially lost function during the initial incident, and that situation is fairly permanent. I also have a little bit of a problem on my right side to this day. I try to mask it about as much as I can. In all candor, there's been a lot of improvement regarding those two areas. After a while, it became better for me to just get out a little bit more and to think a little more clearly. I never stopped trying to improve my speech.

After the five weeks at Magee, I was able to walk better. That took place just as Philadelphia was about to welcome Pope Francis I into the city for his heralded visit. All I could think about was having him nearby. The Pope being here helped me with my faith. It just gave me hope that I could get better. Just thinking about the Pope and how close he was to me at that time just made a spiritual difference for me because I always believed that I was going to get better.

When it came to speech therapy, it took a lot of diligence to get through the daily three-hour sessions. The folks who do the occupational therapy work are to be highly commended. This went on for the better part of the year. At the same time, the strength in my legs was coming back. I spent a lot of time on a balance machine. You have to stay with it. You want to make sure you don't stumble, fall, and hit your head again. All the other stuff— like weightlifting, bike riding—was helpful, too. I started getting more active with the physical stuff.

To assist with my speech therapy, I read a lot of newspapers out loud. That helped quite a bit. Now comes a little secret—while I was at Magee, some very friendly, cooperative folks let me rollerblade down in the basement hallways with a leash, a stick, and a hockey helmet. Quite a kick! The hallways were mostly empty, so you could really rev it up if you wanted to. That's when I knew I was going to be OK. If I could do this I could pretty much do anything. I could tell I had better balance. And I didn't have to think about it so much; it was starting to come naturally again.

CHAPTER 27

THE MIRACLE MACHINES

TECHNOLOGY CAN BE A BEAUTIFUL THING, especially when all the body parts aren't quite synchronized. After my stroke, the rehabilitation effort required more than just a personal work ethic. There's where some auxiliary assistance helped out a lot.

One of the most beneficial pieces of equipment is something that's been around for quite some time. The hyperbaric chamber, also known as a sensory deprivation tank, has a number of benefits. My personal experience with this device started back in 2018 when I crossed paths with a company called Oxygen Oasis, led by CEO Victoria Bliss. Hyperbaric oxygen therapy appealed to me, and I began participating in 40 sessions of 90 minutes each. As a stroke victim, I found it to have remarkable healing qualities. It's a holistic approach to improving mental clarity and enhancing productivity.

Hyperbaric oxygen therapy is really good for high-performing athletes who are looking to improve through oxygen enhancement in the tank. Other benefits include the reduction of inflammation and improvement of cognitive function in the brain. It took me about three months to complete the 40 sessions. I tried to do about four or five sessions every week. At the start, I really noticed a big difference. I was thinking more clearly, my sleeping improved, and everything seemed to be in sharper focus. Also, my reaction time picked up. I noticed improvement in my speech. Getting oxygen into your blood helps a lot.

Another product I found helpful was a special kind of sock from the company VoxxLife, which I've been using for a few years. It involves vibrotactile technology. It combines the best technology with wellness. The best part about it is, of course, it's drug-free and non-invasive, so you don't have to worry about side effects or anything like that. There are all sorts of socks, including the popular compression ones. When I first learned about this, I wore the socks every day. I discovered the technology works. There's a pattern woven into the sock that sort of helps you with your balance. You can run better, recover faster. I've given some to my family members and they notice a big difference. They realized this when they stood in one place (like at a bar) for a considerable amount of time—say, for eight hours. They noticed less fatigue, better balance, and just an overall greater sense of wellness.

The numbers tell the story—athletes reported a 22 percent improvement in power and 30 percent improvement in balance.

Another very helpful device is the BEMER machine. I bought one in 2017, about two years after the incident. I've been using it every day, and that's probably the best endorsement of a product you can make. As for its benefits, right at the top of the list is blood flow enhancement. The BEMER, which stands for Bio Electro Magnetic Energy Regulation, provides upwards of 30 percent improvement in how blood circulates through your body. Without sounding too much like a spokesman for the company, I can tell you unequivocally that I have not gotten sick, I have tons of energy, I sleep better, I think more clearly, I talk better, and I've progressed in other areas, too.

The BEMER is a consumer medical device that sends a low-intensity pulsed electromagnetic field to the body to safely stimulate healthy muscles during an eight-minute session. This temporarily enhances local blood flow to better disperse oxygen throughout the tissues and eliminate CO_2. Additional benefits include reduced stress, improved relaxation, optimized physical performance, enhanced muscle conditioning, and physical fitness.

You lie on this mat with a little computer attached. Personally, I use the thing eight minutes in the morning and then eight more minutes at night. It takes a while to adjust to the product, so I started at level four and stayed with that a week. Then I moved up to level five for another week, followed by six and then finally seven. But you have to stay with it and progress steadily. The idea is to clear your body of toxins, which in my case is highly important.

When you use this device the right way, it makes a big difference. It's safe to say that this plays a role in my ability to continue to play sports such as hockey and golf. A lot of athletes use the BEMER, too; it's even helpful for people who don't have major health issues. The rationale: Everyone has capillaries, which need good blood flow, and that's the main purpose of the BEMER technology.

I know there are a lot of cyclists who use it, but athletes in football, hockey, and other sports probably should use it because of the numerous benefits. I swear by it because I've seen the results.

With all these sophisticated devices, patience is key. Cutting corners or not spending the prescribed amount of time with them will produce mixed results. Keep in mind, extensive studies have been conducted on almost every one of these products. To get maximum benefits, it's good to stick to the recommended plan of action.

Hockey is a sport that relies so much on blood flow and oxygen intake. If you don't have the stamina and the overall fitness to execute a high-quality 45-second shift in lower levels of professional hockey, chances are you're not going to make it to the National Hockey League and stay there.

My only regret is we didn't have the benefits of all these mechanical enhancements when I was a player. It most likely would have made the job a whole lot easier. There were times when we played a home game one night and a road game the very next day. We surely could have used some help in the third period of that second game. That's around the time everyone started looking up at the clock because the game just couldn't end fast enough.

———————

When people learn that I suffered a stroke the better part of a decade ago, curiosity often gets the best of them. They ask questions about my recovery—how did I get better, how did I improve, how much rehab does one go through, and how long does it take for your brain to get better and to heal?

The thing is, no two people are alike, and no two strokes are alike. I often answer those questions by preaching patience. It's going to take time, because the healing of the brain doesn't work on a set schedule. What we do know about a common denominator for a return to good brain health is it's going to take, in most cases, a long time to heal.

So the first question I ask in the way of answer is, how long ago did the survivor have his or her particular incident? How did it happen and what did it affect? That's because some of these people have been in recovery for a few years. Every once in a while you will come across a person who had an incident fairly recently. I tell them they can call me whenever they want and then I try to give them some advice.

It's important to note that the period up to about three months after a stroke is the most important for recovery. That's when survivors see the most improvement. From what I've read, during that three-month period most patients will enter and complete an inpatient rehabilitation program or make progress in their therapy sessions.

In my case, the goal of my rehabilitation was to restore my function as close to pre-stroke levels as possible or to develop compensation strategies to work around a functional impairment. According to an article on this subject published by the Mayo Clinic in Minnesota, an example of a compensation strategy is learning to hold a tube of toothpaste so the strong hand can unscrew the top.

I find that thinking games can be a big help when it comes to later recovery. We play Scrabble and other games that require your brain to dig a little deeper for answers. I used to read newspapers out loud, which I still do. That sort of exercise is really good for brain function. It makes you think to do something like that.

On the physical side of things, I try to do weights as much as I can. We winter in Florida, so one of my routines is a daily four-mile walk on the beach. We also have a hot sauna that I use for about an hour per day. That helps the thinking process. At one point we decided to get a Peloton treadmill, which always gets me to run or walk for cardiovascular fitness.

Anything that keeps you moving can be beneficial. A stationary bicycle mounted on a stand in the basement can go easier on your body because you're sitting down and there's less strain on your back and legs. Plus, you don't have to concentrate on your movements as much on a stationary bike and makes it easier to watch television or listen to music.

Playing golf might not be viewed as the greatest form of exercise, but it does get you out in the fresh air and thinking about strategy for each shot. As anyone knows, it can be time consuming, so that helps pass the time while you're doing something productive.

Naturally, I love to ice skate, and you don't have to play hockey to enjoy it. Go to a public session at a rink and just hear the shouts of joy and laughter. Adults sometimes act like little kids. If there's a healthier activity to get the lungs working a little harder, I haven't found it.

I can tell you from experience that you are always rehabbing. There's no getting around it—not if you want to keep your mental and physical faculties working at full speed. I tell people to never give up. As mentioned earlier, that's what I told people at Bancroft. Not everyone is the same. I was an athlete, so I believe that led to a slightly above-average time for getting back to where I was prior to my stroke. Some people get frustrated. They give up rather than just keeping up with it. It takes determination to stay with a program. The idea is to have a goal to make as a full a recovery as your body and brain will allow.

Stay positive. Your recovery is counting on that.

CHAPTER 28

LOVE OF MY LIFE

W E'VE SPENT A LOT OF TIME reviewing how I managed to survive and recover from my 2015 stroke through hard work and a never-give-up attitude. But to completely come back, I needed a life partner, and I was very lucky to find such a person.

I had known Eileen's family for a number of years. I'd known her brother, Bill McCay, for upwards of 40 years because he had been the photographer for my Make-A-Wish charity tournament (1990–94) at the Blue Heron Pines Golf Club down near the Jersey Shore. Bill has four sisters—Eileen, Kathleen, Colleen, and Maureen. Bill was running his own golf tournament for six years at Ramblewood Country Club in Mount Laurel, New Jersey. Eileen was a volunteer at the event, and Colleen was with her.

Eileen has a great smile, she's easy to talk with about any subject, and she has a great attitude regarding charity work. She stayed until the very end of that tournament. I had a chance to have a conversation with her that day and got to know her a little better. That night I told her I had a BEMER machine, which, as I mentioned, helps with the blood flow in your entire body. By then I had owned the device for the better part of five years and could vouch for its effectiveness. So, I loaned it to Eileen for two weeks when I was back home visiting my family in Saskatchewan.

She tried it, and that's how I was able to connect with her. We started dating in 2018 and, like any sound relationship, we needed to have trust in one another. We had both been through prior relationships that had not worked out. Right off, we communicated very well, laughed a lot, and built trust with each other. It was nice to get to know her throughout 2019 and then, in 2020, COVID hit. So we ended up spending a lot of time together. I had been living in an apartment in Pennsauken, New Jersey. We decided to buy a house together in nearby Haddonfield.

You can guess how the story went from there. We got married on September 26, 2020, in a backyard ceremony in Haddonfield. Quite a day. I met the whole family and got along with everybody well. Eileen's mom was a real firecracker, all of five feet tall, and loved to dance and be with people. What a sense of humor! I had a chance to meet her when Eileen and I were first dating. Her mom was living with Eileen's sister, Maureen. I visited her mom in the hospital when she had a hip problem. Her hands were cold, so I held one of them for half an hour. She liked that so much that she pinched one of my cheeks with affection. I was smiling and, as I was leaving, she called me "pink cheeks." We had a good laugh over that one.

Eileen has really helped me in my quest to get back to a strong semblance of what I was before 2015. She's always looking for ways to get my right hand to function better. I always wake up with a smile and an awesome attitude, always positive, which makes me thankful to be alive. I remind myself I could have died. We've been working for the last year to build the franchise Prime IV Hydration & Wellness in Marlton, New Jersey. It should really help a lot of people who need this sort of thing.

Everything I do now seems better when Eileen participates with me. We play golf a little bit more. In my early adulthood I could hit the ball a long way. At the start, when I had my stroke,

I could only hit the ball about 75 yards. Now I can hit it over 200 and usually pretty straight. I'm about a 16 handicap, which is somewhat higher than my younger days. But now it's all about having fun and going out for a day outdoors. I am involved in a lot of charity events. In Florida, we have a group of guys who play from 7 to 10 AM. It is a course with mostly par-3 holes and a couple par-4s. The best part is it is nice and warm. You do not have to worry about the weather.

Now here is something that might amuse you. I play barefoot, and I tell people I can do that because I am always in the fairway. Things are a little more relaxed down there when it comes to attire. Other golfers see me, and I guess they are thinking, *That is a little different.* I like the freedom of feeling the ground. The days of serious spikes are over. As for hockey, I can still play pretty well. We have a morning league in Pennsauken that plays every Wednesday and Friday. Every once in a while, I'll come back and play with those guys. Just about 10 a side. It makes me happy; I'm so thankful to be alive and to play hockey. I love that every time out. It is a joy to be able to still do some of the things I love.

This much I am sure of—when you have a partner in life, it just makes everything more meaningful. You can better appreciate the joys and sorrows, the ups and downs, the highs and lows when you have a trusted companion by your side. When something noteworthy happens, you can look over at your special someone to gauge their reaction. Sometimes it might validate a decision you make or sometimes it might give you pause for thought and possibly change your mind—for the better, of course.

In the time after the stroke, I had experienced numerous moments when I had mixed feelings about the future. But in recent years, those brief instances when I may have lacked confidence have diminished, and much of the credit for that goes to Eileen. She seems to sense when those encouraging words are needed and when to let life take its course. It's great to know I can just be myself and not have to worry too much about what people might think of me. That includes going barefoot on the golf course.

The support I get from Eileen really does make a difference. She does not pressure me to do anything. She says, "Go ahead and do whatever you need to do and be a happy guy." So, again, I am thankful for all of that. I truly am blessed, and it makes me think that someone really is watching over me.

CHAPTER 29

COLLEGE VS. JUNIOR

F I HAD A DOLLAR for every time I heard the debate about the best route to take to the NHL—college vs. junior hockey—I could retire and take the first plane to Tahiti. Of course, the answer is there is no answer. Both are great ways for a young player to prepare for the professional game. The level of competition in both arenas of play has never been better.

I came up through the junior ranks with the Brandon Wheat Kings. As I was advancing through my late teenage years, the NHL draft age minimum was still 20, so it gave people like me a little more time to mature. Now players get taken at 18 and, on television on draft day, some of them don't look like they've started shaving yet.

Things haven't really changed all that much over the last 40-plus years since my career got underway. Junior hockey, much of it based in Canada, was more physical than college back in the '80s, and I would say that still holds true today. College hockey is a slightly faster brand of hockey.

Funny thing is, right after the year I was drafted, the NHL lowered the age by two years. Everything changed. Players in junior hockey were much younger. They were a little more immature. Kids were playing at 16 and 17. There was a lot going on when

I was that age. The NHL-rival World Hockey Association was still around in those days, and that was something to consider. I was aware that a lot of players had a choice to make. If I had gone that route, I know I could have played at 18 or 19 and been a good player. But a bunch of us on Brandon, including Brad McCrimmon and Ray Allison, wanted to stay around one more year to make a try for the Memorial Cup (we came up just short, losing to Peterborough in the final).

I'm sure I was ready to play pro at 18 because I was already one of the best players in the Western Hockey League. That wouldn't have been a problem for me.

The difference between college and junior is it's nice to have a start in your advanced education and working toward a degree, particularly when you think about your post-hockey years and what you're going to make of yourself in another line of work. I think it's great if you can get a start on your education first. Plus, it's easy to see they're more mature. Backing up your hockey career with a degree can be helpful because, let's face it, the years of chasing pucks usually end sometime in your thirties.

From a style standpoint, to contrast the two hockey feeder systems most often depends on each individual player. Take the Flyers' Bobby Brink and Tyson Foerster, for example. Both forwards made the Philadelphia 2023–24 season-opening roster. Brink, who captured an NCAA Division I scoring crown while playing for Denver University, made a strong impression right away with his foot speed and his playmaking ability in NHL competition. His middle name is Orr, so why would you expect anything less?

Foerster is more the power forward type. He played his junior hockey for the Barrie Colts of the Ontario Hockey League. At 6'2", 200 pounds, he can push his way through defensemen rather than try to skate around them. It took him the better part of 20 games to get his first goal in the 2023–24 season, but once he got that first one, the rest started coming in bunches.

When you compare the list of all-time alums from college vs. junior, it's not even close.

Here are my top 10 junior grads:

1. Bobby Orr, Oshawa
2. Mario Lemieux, Laval
3. Guy Lafleur, Quebec
4. Bobby Clarke, Flin Flon
5. Mike Bossy, Laval
6. Eric Lindros, Oshawa
7. Sidney Crosby, Rimouski
8. Denis Potvin, Ottawa
9. John Tavares, Oshawa
10. Pat LaFontaine, Verdun

Now, not taking anything away from college guys, but here's my list of them:

1. Jonathan Toews, University of North Dakota
2. Patrick Sharp, University of Vermont
3. Zach Parise, University of North Dakota
4. Tim Thomas, University of Vermont
5. Paul Stastny, University of Denver
6. Duncan Keith, Michigan State University
7. Dany Heatley, University of Wisconsin
8. Brian Gionta, Boston College
9. Martin St. Louis, University of Vermont
10. Phil Kessel, University of Minnesota

Nowadays, a handful of 18-year-olds at or near the top of the draft can make the transition right into the NHL. Others will have to wait, either staying in college for another year or perhaps signing a pro contract and playing in places like the American Hockey League. It might take a year or two to mature both on and off the ice before they can make the jump.

Our former Flyers captain Dave Poulin was ready to play for Notre Dame after he went undrafted. He played four years for the Fighting Irish and by the time he graduated he was more than ready to play in the NHL. Actually, he first went to play in Sweden, where he was coached by Ted Sator, who just happened to be a scout for the Flyers. He recommended Poulin be added to the Philadelphia roster and what a great tip that was. Dave went on to have a great career in the NHL. On our team he fit in well, and when the coach decided to have him center a line with Tim Kerr and myself, it clicked right away.

From what I see of college and junior hockey now, it's not as physical as when we played. There's a greater emphasis on speed and skill. Maybe that's what the fans want, but all I know is when an occasional body-bumping game breaks out, the arena starts to get real loud and everyone in the stands is smiling.

––––––––––

Nothing comes easy when women athletes try to break the glass ceiling and strive to have competitions that determine the sport's best. Nowhere is this more evident than in the Olympics ice hockey movement, which didn't earn the right to hand out medals in competition until 1998 at the Winter Games in Nagano, Japan.

I've always appreciated what it takes for female skaters to compete in a physically demanding sport such as ice hockey. It requires more body contact than basketball, it's much faster than softball, and I'm not sure something like flag football deserves to be mentioned in the same sentence with the ice crew.

For years, Canada dominated women's hockey mainly because there was much more access to natural ice, plus other sports such as basketball did not have quite the same appeal as they did in the United States. After time, the Americans got much better, as evidenced by their surprise gold medal at Nagano. However, Canada won the next four gold medals at Salt Lake City in 2002; Turin, Italy, in 2006; Vancouver in 2010; and Sochi, Russia, in 2014. The U.S. took gold at PyeongChang, Korea, in 2018, but Canada bounced right back to the top of the podium at Beijing, China, in 2022.

The rest of the world? It has a lot of catching up to do. It's still a two-horse race. That's why you see so many lopsided scores in the Olympic Games, except when Canada and the United States play each other.

There have been attempts made to start a women's professional hockey league, such as the Canadian Women's Hockey League (CWHL), which started in 2007, and the National Women's Hockey League, which started in 2015 and changed names and configurations many times. The CWHL incorporated some American teams and in 2009 started giving the champion the Clarkson Cup, which was donated to the league by governor general Adrienne Clarkson in the same spirit Lord Stanley donated a trophy for men's hockey in 1892.

I recall the year 2010 because that was the year the Hockey Hall of Fame in Toronto first started inducting women into the shrine. Cammi Granato and Angela James were the first honorees.

The CWHL folded in 2019 and that left Canadian, American, and European players without a meaningful place to compete. However, the new Professional Women's Hockey League (PWHL) got underway in January 2024.

A lot of people are hoping the PWHL catches on and that the North American hockey fan base jumps on board the way the basketball community did when the WNBA was started. For one thing, young female players will have role models that they can both learn from and emulate. The idea is to expand the talent pool so that there are both more and better players from which to choose.

At the same time, women's hockey holds a lot of potential from a skill standpoint. Just like the contrast between men's and women's basketball—where most men can dunk and execute power moves and few women can—the same kind of holds true for hockey. Women rely more on crafty passing and playmaking. There aren't as many headbanging checks in front of the net or in the corners. Fighting? Not really a factor. When's the last time you saw two women players drop the gloves and really go at it? And if the pro game catches on, there will be a need for more qualified women's coaches. Which is the way it should be.

The Hockey Hall of Fame allows the induction of two women per year. Until the sport gets more competitive, the Hall might want to go with just one woman for now. At the moment, the only players deserving of such an honor either come from Team Canada or Team USA. There just isn't a whole lot of competition from the rest of the world. The new pro league could grow the talent base, but it's going to take some time before it has the depth to rival even men's minor league hockey. There just aren't as many development opportunities as there are with the WNBA.

One area where there has been a lot of progress is in women's officiating. Laura White of South Jersey is one of about a dozen female referees who have advanced as far as officiating male players in the American Hockey League. She also worked some in-house scrimmages at Philadelphia Flyers training camp in 2023. White knows the game. Today's men's game is easier for women refs because there's more skating and it's not quite as physical as it once was. I think she would do a good job in the NHL because she knows hockey and it would be nice to see if a female referee could handle this demanding challenge.

NHL commissioner Gary Bettman believes women are making advances in this area and gives the impression a female official might someday work in his league, just as they have in the NBA and NFL. I believe it's only a matter of time.

CHAPTER 30

GENE HART

G ENE WAS GREAT FRIENDS with all the Flyers players, and a lot of them came along well after he was into his announcing career. The thing about Gene was that when he said, "How are you doing?" he really wanted to know how you were doing. He was that kind of guy, someone who wanted to get to know a person beyond just the usual casual inquiry.

That came through on his broadcasts. He often shared personal anecdotes in on-air conversations with longtime partners Stu Nahan, Don Earle, and Bobby Taylor, best known as serving as Bernie Parent's competent backup through some of the glory years.

When it came to announcers, Hart knew a lot more about worldly subjects than most. Right from the start of my career I grew to like him, and it all began when my parents visited nearby NHL cities such as Winnipeg, Edmonton, and Calgary to watch me play when the Flyers hit town. Being a minister, my dad loved talking with Hart. Both were the kind of people who wanted to know how everyone was doing, where they lived, what they did for a living.

Gene was a master at weaving that information into his radio or TV shows. Some people said he bled Flyers orange. Helping others was one of Gene's passions. When I started my charity golf tournament in the early '90s at Blue Heron Pines in South Jersey, he was one of the first to volunteer his time for the Make-A-Wish Foundation event.

He had several signature lines, including, "He scores, he scores for a case of Tastykakes!" That was a reference to a Philadelphia-area treat. During the Stanley Cup quests in the 1970s, the goal call became almost a standard for youngsters throughout the Delaware Valley. Each player who first scored a goal was awarded a case of the yummy Tastykakes. Currently, the case of Tastykakes is given to the favorite charity of that particular player who scores first.

At the end of games, Gene's signoff line was "Good night and good hockey!" That became a standard for a lot of hockey fans when they bid good night to a fellow player, relative, or friend.

Prior to announcing, Gene was a master of all trades. After graduating from Trenton State College with a degree in education and serving in the military, he embarked on a career as a high school sports official, overseeing games in football, baseball, and basketball in South Jersey. When Atlantic City High School athletic broadcaster Ralph Glenn needed someone to go with him to Trenton to announce a game, Gene agreed, and his announcing career was born.

While all that was going on, Gene served as a history teacher for a couple years. When Philadelphia was granted an expansion franchise to be called the Flyers, he submitted some tapes to the team. Since the Flyers couldn't afford a more experienced announcer, Gene got the job. At first he thought it would be only a temporary position. But he was so well received that he stayed on for 29 years, including six Stanley Cup Finals and two championships.

In the late '90s, when the Flyers showed an interest in me as an analyst on radio broadcasts, I had virtually no experience. That's when Gene, who was retired by then, helped me out by listening to my tapes. He gave me some advice and that made a big difference for me. After all, I was learning from the best.

Another favorite memory of Gene I have goes back to the early '80s when we would bus to New York City to play the Rangers. He would sit in the front seat with the rest of the broadcast crew. If we won, there was always a lot of good-spirited teasing and kidding going on. Gene's favorite target was Bob "the Hound" Kelly. Bob was good-natured but that only made him more of a foil for Gene's humor. He had the whole bus cracking up. Bob would try to gallantly fire back at Gene's jabs, but it was a losing battle. Gene always got the best of him. One of Gene's favorite lines was, "It's easy to spot Kelly's name on the Stanley Cup, it's the one written in crayon!"

There are plenty of Hart stories to go around. There's the one about how he met his wife, Sarah. She was the daredevil who sat atop a horse on a tower along the Steel Pier in Atlantic City. As the spellbound audience watched, she would prod the horse to jump straight down into what amounted to a tank of water. Now that caught Gene's eye! But it was a dangerous circus act, and it eventually was closed down for good by animal rights activists in 1993. It was something that bordered on crazy and that you would never dream of doing now.

After a career like Gene's, induction into the Hockey Hall of Fame was a foregone conclusion. The ceremony for his accepting the Foster Hewitt Memorial Award was well received. In addition to hockey, he also called harness racing at local horse tracks.

One of Gene's greatest loves was the opera. He could tell you the plot of just about any famous performance. He could recite lines in different languages and even do so in appropriate accents.

If that wasn't impressive enough, he could knock off the *Los Angeles Times* crossword puzzle in 15 minutes. I couldn't believe it. I was lucky if I could get even a couple clues and by then he would be done. As they say in that hobby, he did them in ink, not pencil. That's how good he was.

This much I can tell you—when it came to enthusiasm for the call of a game, Gene never took a night off. He could make a dull November game sound like Game 7 of the Stanley Cup Final.

Because he had so many interests and had such a good memory, he could weave little stories into his broadcasts. That could be why he developed such a strong local following.

By now, there are plenty of people who weren't around to hear Gene's famous final call when the Flyers won their first championship in 1974 against Bobby Orr in the Bruins. I recommend they find some video of that announcement. "The Flyers win the Stanley Cup! The Flyers win the Stanley Cup!" For the big celebration and the parade down Broad Street, Gene sported perhaps the biggest smile of all and received a lot of cheers. It's one of the finest days in Philadelphia sports history and Gene was squarely in the middle of it all.

Gene passed away in 1999 but his legacy lives on through his daughter Lauren Hart, a professional recording artist who performs "The Star-Spangled Banner" (and "O Canada" when a team north of the border is in town) before all Flyers home games. She also performs a duet of "God Bless America" along with the late Kate Smith via videotape before big games such as the 2010 Stanley Cup Final. She often wears a jersey with No. 68 on it to honor the age of her father when he died.

Lauren does a great job with that. No doubt some of the depth and power of her voice comes from her famous father. Several months ago, her husband, Todd Carmichael, suffered a mini stroke, and I was able to speak with him about that at one of the Flyers' charity events. I told him to keep up the hope, stay diligent with his rehab. It can make a big difference. He travels all over the world, has a number of children, and hasn't slowed down a bit.

In conclusion, I really loved Gene and his family. It came as no surprise when they dedicated the Wells Fargo Center press box in his honor. That's how much he meant to all those fortunate enough to know him.

In my eyes, too many hockey players used to want to have their career "cake" and eat it too. By that, I mean professional athletes thought they could get by following a less-than-ideal diet and then perform at a high level. Some may have gotten by with that approach early in their tenure, but eventually it caught up to them. For example, you can't include a steady intake of beer and the like past your early twenties or you are setting yourself up for premature retirement.

Like a lot of young players, I didn't realize an intake of substandard food can have a negative impact on where you're trying to go. When I first came into the league, I had no real clue about physical fitness. Then came 1981 and the arrival of one Pat Croce, a physical trainer whose mission in life seemed to be to help others get well and get better. He taught the young Flyers the right way to get better. Two of his most loyal followers were Tim Kerr and Dave Poulin. Kerr put together four straight 50-goal seasons and Poulin became our inspirational captain, who once scored a goal three-on-five against Quebec in the 1985 playoffs.

A better diet and a more efficient workout program probably added about three years to my career. Overall I felt better, and it didn't take as long for me to recover after the games. Croce was the man behind all that. He made believers out of most of us. He had his own facility in Pennsylvania, so if you were injured and needed treatment, you had to head on over there from New

Jersey. Let me just say that Pat was as competitive as they come and really hated to lose.

Most of the stuff we did was of a cross-training nature. Pat was a big believer in things like bicycling. Only his workouts were a lot faster than any of us were used to. Thing is, he could ride with the best of us so there were no wisecracks or rolling eyes.

From 1980, my diet, along with everyone else's, underwent a real overhaul. In those days—the late '70s, early '80s—there was beer in the refrigerator in or near the locker room for after games. In Philly, that was the case until Pelle Lindbergh's tragic alcohol-related death in 1985.

Admittedly, we hadn't been eating that well. I know when I first started in the NHL, a pregame meal was something like a big steak, salad, and pasta—a lot of heavy stuff. We were 21 or 22 and believed we were bulletproof. As I got older, I didn't eat as much. More salad calories, fewer fat ones. You learn as the years go by. Pat had something to do with that. He also taught how weightlifting as a fitness tool was an efficient and natural way to control your body mass. He showed us how to do it the right way, which is so important. A lot of guys who don't do it correctly end up with an injury or just don't get as much out of the workout as they should.

I know that it made a big difference for us, especially at the tail end of games or on a long road trip with a lot of travel. The fatigue can get to you but if you're in top shape you can lessen the consequences. A lot of times when you are on the road, you can do some weights in your hotel room to keep up. As the game's speed picked up in the '90s, I found out you had to be even more conscientious. Every year at training camp they had footraces, usually in the vicinity of a couple miles. I'll admit I wasn't a good runner, and for this sort of conditioning exercise it didn't matter that I was a good player. I and others hated to

run so they added a bike test. That was a little easier on the
back and legs.

Now it's much different. Everyone has their own personal
trainer. Regimens are customized to each athlete's needs. The
diet is superb food. Personal chefs abound. But they don't have
as much fun, that's for sure, because we used to drink our share
of beer and the like.

Rest is important too, and that includes sleep. Problems can
arise on the road because players, especially the younger ones,
have to share rooms. Not everyone is a quiet sleeper. Some guys,
like the late Brad McCrimmon and Mark Howe, hit it off right
away, in part because they were defense partners on the ice. So no
doubt they would be up late at night going over strategy. But there
are guys who are world-champion snorers. They can drown out
a good high school football band. When that happens, they have
to get their own room. I know I was a bad snorer and so there
were some allowances made. Nowadays, if a player is a veteran
of a certain number of years or games, they get their own room.

In the 1980 first-round series against Edmonton, "Moose"
Dupont was my roommate. I'll never forget that he smoked cigarettes in the room and loved watching cartoons early in the
morning on television. Just picture it—a 220-pound man sitting
in a chair with no shirt on puffing on a butt and watching *Felix
the Cat*! To say that was a challenge, well, you can finish that
sentence yourself.

If you aren't old enough to have seen Moose play hockey, you
should get your hands on some video. The guy was a piece of
work. He would knock some opponent's socks off, then skate over
to the bench with a big grin on his face. From what I've been
told, he was the perfect foil for Shero. If Moose wasn't trying
hard enough in a half-rink drill in practice, the coach would have
Moose skate to the other end of the ice and do push-ups. Only

thing was, Moose would just do these goofy half push-ups and the guys on the bench would be howling with laughter. Freddie would pretend to be in one of his notorious "fogs," but he knew what was going on.

Also, Moose was known for his crazy "Moose Shuffle" dance step after scoring a goal. Of course, even though he didn't score the winning (and only) goal in Game 6 of the 1974 victory over Boston in the Cup-clincher, he was the one who shot the puck that "Hawk" MacLeish tipped in. Holy Kate Smith! Moose's knees were churning so fast, people's eyes were having a hard time keeping up.

In today's game, everyone flies in charter jets. That wasn't always the case back in the '80s. It's awesome, because you play a game in a far-off city, then you jump on a jet later that night, fly home, and wake up in your own bed. Back in the day you had to fly commercial. It was kind of difficult because it was tough to relax or move around to see and speak to other guys.

Playing in Philadelphia, we didn't fly as much as some of the teams out west did. We were able to take trains or buses to a lot of away games in the conference. Nowadays, long distance flights aren't as daunting because they have the whole plane to themselves.

One season I missed more than 20 games with a knee injury. Croce put me through a grueling rehab program. The last thing I wanted to see was another piece of heavy iron or Pat yelling, "Just one more!" But when it was over, I could feel the overall difference.

———————

Progressive thinkers like Flyers former head trainer Pat Croce steered a lot of athletes on the right road to good fitness. In some ways, he was well ahead of his time. He and I had a good relationship partly because I never had a problem with my weight.

In my playing years I was in the vicinity of 188 pounds, and I'm still around that now. I didn't go up and down like some guys did. I tried to watch what I ate, especially in-season. You have to reach a certain balance when it comes to carbohydrates or types of food that might contain more fat percentage than is productive to high-level fitness.

My pal, the late Brad McCrimmon, was one of those players who could put on an extra 20 or so pounds in the summer and then would somehow manage to drop most or all of it before training camp started. Now most of the players don't have such pronounced highs and lows. They have their own personal chefs who prepare all their food, which is a lot different than the old days.

Sleep is important for hockey players because it's such a physically demanding sport. You might only play around 20 minutes a night, but your time on the ice is basically nonstop. By 45 seconds or a minute on a shift, you're usually winded because you're skating at a high tempo. The last thing you need to be is fatigued from a bad (or short) night in the sack. These days I use that aforementioned BEMER machine. I wish I'd had that during my playing days. It really helps you get a restful night of shut-eye. The BEMER assists with energy and sleeping without interruption throughout the night. It makes the whole process a lot easier.

When I was a player I loved my afternoon nap. It was really part of my routine, whether we were playing at home or on the road. The morning skate can take a little something out of you and the last thing you need to feel is tired going into a big game. So generally we would practice in the morning, have a pregame meal a little after 12 PM, and then nap between 2 and 4 PM. I could sleep through a thunderstorm, so that hour or two checking out the backs of my eyelids was never a problem. Some guys don't nap too much, but I'm guessing the majority of them still do. By the way, everyone can thank former Flyers assistant coach Mike Nykoluk for "inventing" the morning skate. Before 1973, hardly any NHL teams came near a hockey rink the morning of a game, but Nykoluk convinced head coach Fred Shero this was a good idea and after the Flyers won a couple Cups, the idea stuck.

On non-game days in which teams work out at their practice rinks, there's a certain degree of off-ice training but weightlifting is not as prominent as one might be led to believe. There's been an evolution to more ergonomic stuff, including running and flexibility/stretching exercises.

From what I gather, drinking is down from when my generation played. With much bigger contracts, there's more on the line than just playing the game for glory and good times. Some players constantly search websites to find out about the latest nutrition and fitness tips.

At our fledgling company, Prime IV Hydration, intravenous drips figure prominently in new ways to get nutrition into one's system. Hydration and getting full use of vitamins and supplements are quite helpful in achieving high performance levels. A number of professional football players have been experimenting with drips as a more efficient way to get important elements into their systems. If it works for them, it should work for the guys on skates.

———————

Perhaps one of the most underrated ways of improving performance both in sports and regular life is proper hydration. Not only do enhancing fluids keep your internal levels at peak efficiency, they also help with carrying vitamins, supplements, and preventive medicine throughout your body by modern technological intravenous methods.

Our family opened a Prime IV franchise in Marlton, New Jersey, to address this issue. There were about a hundred franchises already in existence when we started and another hundred or so were on the planning board. The purpose of this movement is to help people look, feel, and perform better. This is especially crucial for athletes in highly demanding sports.

But there are other benefits as well, from anti-aging to weight loss to even hangover recovery. For me, I've been doing some research as this pertains to my stroke recovery. As I've already mentioned, I still play hockey and, now that I'm in my sixties, I can't just take good health for granted. As you get older, you lose cells in your body and so I've taken a long, slow infusion of a substance that should help with that process.

Hydration is important because it's essential for the brain, heart, joints, kidneys, and muscles. That's why you see a lot of water bottles not only below or on the rail in front of the Flyers' bench, because dehydration can definitely cause performance to slip.

CHAPTER 31

FLYERS ALUMNI

FLYERS TEAM FOUNDER Ed Snider was always one to promote the idea of a family concept regarding his players, the coaching staff, and his loyal fan base. Oh, and one other important group: the Flyers Alumni. In recent years, the presence of this growing association has become more active in the Delaware Valley community, helping those less fortunate, providing things like bicycles to worthy young disabled recipients, and generally spreading goodwill throughout the area.

Current alumni president Brad Marsh has done an admirable job connecting former Flyers players with the hockey fan community.

I've been a member of the Flyers organization and its alumni for the better part of five decades, and so I've had a great first-hand look at what the ex-Flyers have done both for the fans and for each other. I've been on the board of directors for 10 years and know pretty much all there is to know about the inner workings of this fraternity. In addition to being a player in Philadelphia for 11 years, I spent nine years in the radio booth helping to call games. Plus, I've been an ambassador along with my good friend Bernie Parent, the Hall of Fame goaltender who won the Conn Smythe Trophy as MVP in both of the Cup years. Also, Dave

Schultz was involved with community outreach for four years before COVID struck.

Basically, you're in front of all these fans who want to love you and want to be a part of what's going on. Some of the activities include the Flyers Charities Carnival (formerly the Flyers Wives Carnival), which is probably the longest-running charity fundraiser of its kind in the National Hockey League. On the main concourse of the Wells Fargo Center, fans are able to test their golf, ping pong, and gaming skills with activations from Topgolf, SPIN Philadelphia, and Nerd Street Gamers. Funds raised from the carnival benefit Flyers Charities and its mission to support a multitude of worthy nonprofit organizations that provide educational and recreational resources to underserved youth, engage in important medical and healthcare research, and promote numerous community investment initiatives to positively influence the community. These organizations include the American Cancer Society, Ed Snider Youth Hockey Foundation & Education, Leukemia & Lymphoma Society, Michael's Way, Philadelphia Ronald McDonald House, Salvation Army, Simon's Heart, and many more.

Another popular activity is our own golf tournament, an event that gets all the guys together to have some fun. We post a lot of information online for the various charities that the Flyers Alumni have. I know a lot of people at companies that give back.

There are a number of ex-Flyers alumni who currently are employed by the Flyers, including goodwill ambassador Bob Kelly, TV analyst Brian Boucher, radio analyst Todd Fedoruk, team president of hockey operations Keith Jones, general manager Danny Brière, special advisor John LeClair, and goodwill ambassador Dave Schultz.

Since I've been associated with the Flyers, I've always known them as an organization that wants to take care of its own. Much of that had to do with Snider, who wanted to give his players a place to be employed (if they desired) after their hockey careers were over. I was one of those.

Jones tells the story of the time he was forced to retire because of a knee injury with one year remaining on his contract. When the press conference to announce the transaction was over, Jones heard his cell phone ring and saw Snider's name on the display. Jones thought the Flyers owner was calling to voice his displeasure because of the expense of paying a player who was leaving the game due to injury.

But no, Snider was calling to say he wanted Jones to stay in the organization and to use his sharp wit and hockey analytical mind on television broadcasts. Jones was on Flyers TV for more than 20 years and now works in the front office. That's the kind of culture the Flyers have developed over the years.

So many ex-Flyers chose to stay and live in the Philadelphia area after their careers were over. It made sense. In addition to having many friends and supporters, alumni members realized this was the best place to live because of business connections and so forth. Plus, many of these guys loved being in Philadelphia. There's just this attitude about the place. In some ways it's a blue-collar town, but at the same time it's sophisticated with a great deal of culture.

The donation of bicycles to youngsters is one of the more worthwhile endeavors. It's really a nice thing to do. You simply cannot buy the precious smiles on those kids' faces when they first climb on to those fancy two-wheelers. It really helps them in their quest to achieve good health.

Everyone who played for the Flyers and stayed in the area loves Philadelphia. They know why they're here because the people who are working with the Flyers make it special. That makes you want to be part of it. As I've said before, they have a great fan base who remain loyal through good times and bad. That includes people from Pennsylvania, New Jersey, and Delaware. Some will drive a hundred miles or more just to watch the Flyers play. It's easy to see, and hear, that people want to be a part of the whole experience.

I think I've done a good job of promoting the Flyers Alumni and it all comes naturally. If you do something for 44 years, you must enjoy it, right? I really enjoy taking photographs with fans and making someone's day. It only takes a second and there are smiles all around. Just talking with someone for a minute can promote a lot of goodwill and get you a presence on Facebook, Instagram, and X (formerly Twitter).

So for me, it's always been special to be part of the Flyers Alumni. I played in a few other cities at the end of my NHL career, but Philly is my second home after my native Saskatchewan. I love what I do, and that position has a lot to do with helping people.

CHAPTER 32

EQUIPMENT IMPROVEMENTS

ICE HOCKEY IS JUST LIKE any other professional sport. It's fast-moving, often involves contact, and constantly looks for technological ways for equipment to get lighter, more aerodynamic, and less cumbersome. Who hasn't seen an old photograph of a football player in one of those prehistoric leather helmets with no face bar? How about the days when there were no batting helmets in baseball? Or those clunky sneakers in basketball that hindered players from running fast or jumping high for rebounds.

In hockey, advances have been made throughout the years. Wooden sticks are as obsolete as pay telephone booths. Now everyone is playing with lightweight carbon-fiber doozies at $200 a pop. A generation ago, skates could be had for $99. Now you're lucky if you can find a decent pair for under five hundred bucks a pair.

I can say without reservation that when I played, the equipment was not really good. The shin pads would tend to slide or get loose, so you had to use extra tape to keep them in place. Elbow pads weren't much better. They usually were held in place by a strip of elastic. As soon as the play got intense, they slid down your arm, so you had to occasionally pull them back into place. I know that when I was in junior hockey, I had a lot of trouble with my elbows.

If you got hit just the right way, there was nothing funny about having your funny bone lit up. Not a pleasant feeling.

If you look at photographs of players from my era, the shoulder pads were downright dinky. Watching NHL hockey on television, I noticed Montreal legend Yvan Cournoyer wore as little equipment as possible and what he did wear was small. The belief was you could go faster if you were lighter. They didn't call him "the Roadrunner" for nothing. He even went to the trouble of having his skate blades customized to a slightly longer length to enhance his speed. Most skates had steel blades and were made out of pure leather. Those really slowed you down.

The sticks also weren't ideal for quick shots or stickhandling. Companies like Northland and CCM did the best they could with what they had to work with, namely old-fashioned wood. Now they're all composite and one-piece. Slap shots easily go more than 100 miles per hour. Sticks weigh a lot less, so they don't become a burden late in games.

Hockey pants were probably the most efficient pieces of equipment of a bygone era. Even in the '70s and '80s, they had excellent padding and gradually got better at repelling moisture. Now, the helmets were a different story. Fans of a certain age can't help but remember that old contraption Butch Goring wore with the Islanders during their Stanley Cup years in the early '80s. I don't think that instrument provided much protection. Of course, Wayne Gretzky also wore a very lightweight helmet early in his career. Maybe that's why he was so quick. Nobody went out of their way to hit Gretzky that much because he was the guy who was selling tickets. It's safe to say he was lucky there wasn't an accident because the helmet wouldn't have done much to protect him.

Even though Minnesota's Bill Masterton died after striking his head on the ice back in 1968, the movement to get helmets on everyone's heads didn't come along for another decade. The last man to not wear a helmet was former Flyer Craig MacTavish, who didn't retire until 1997. Today's helmets come complete with plastic eye shields. As of April 2023, only about eight holdouts were left around the NHL. When they retire, everyone will have to wear visors.

I've been watching this drama unfold because I have personal experience. I got hit in the eye and it was a scary situation. I knew after that incident I would have to wear a visor to protect my eyes. The one problem a lot of players had was condensation from competing at a high rate and having the visor fog up. Now there are sprays to help keep the shields clear, but you occasionally still see a player reach for a towel to wipe around the inner portion of the plastic for clearer vision.

One thing I was glad to see improve was the material the socks were made of. The wool fabric would get heavy with sweat and make things rather slow and uncomfortable. Believe it or not, garter belts had to be used to keep the socks in place. The new socks are much lighter. Now to perhaps the second most important piece of equipment after the helmet, namely the cup to protect the most vulnerable part of your body. The originals were constructed out of plastic and were held in place by a belt with a pouch. Now it's more of a one-piece deal that keeps the socks and lower-body protection all together in one guard. Again, everything is much lighter and not as cumbersome when you're skating.

Since I still play occasionally, I can appreciate the differences between now and the good, old days. The protection is much more comprehensive and modernized to enhance skating efficiency. A well-struck puck can do some considerable damage, so everything is being done to make the game safer. In late 2023, a hockey player in Europe, Adam Johnson, died after his neck was hit by a skate blade. Several Flyers needed only a week or so to experiment with neck protection devices. Others have been wearing cut-proof tape on their wrists and ankles. I think those are all good moves. Better to be safe than risk a debilitating injury.

CHAPTER 33

NAD TREATMENTS

Wᴵᵀʜᴏᵁᵀ ɢᴇᴛᴛɪɴɢ ᴛᴏᴏ ᴛᴇᴄʜɴɪᴄᴀʟ regarding stroke recovery language, I want to share some information about treatments I tried in late 2023 that produced some very positive results. According to NeuMed, an urgent care facility in Houston, a therapy called nicotinamide adenine dinucleotide (NAD) has shown some encouraging progress in the treatment of serious neurological events like mine. Recent studies confirm NAD, a coenzyme found in all living cells, plays a critical role in cellular energy metabolism, DNA repair, and cellular signaling. Everyone's natural NAD levels begin to decline with age, but they can also be depleted by stress, addiction, and chronic illnesses.

The treatments that I underwent were both extensive and comprehensive. The program consisted of four-hour treatments four times a day for four days. I learned they can really make a big difference. They will try your patience but, as they do in sports, you have to keep your eyes on the prize. I found out these treatments can be invaluable for improved brain regeneration and health, your mood, your memory, recovery of neurological function, and mental clarity.

I noticed a lot of improvement right after completing the program. As I have discussed, one of the big negative side effects of the stroke was the limited use of my right hand, which is my "power" hand. After the NAD sessions, things felt much better in that hand. My fingers worked much better. Before the treatments they were almost locked in a straight-out position. Bending them was next to impossible. But just days after completing the program, my fingers not only felt better but had a much greater range of motion. Likewise my wrist, which has a lot more flexibility.

As far as mental functionality, I've had much improvement there as well. My thinking seems to be clearer and I'm hoping this carries over into more clarity in my speech. There are other benefits to NAD treatments as well. You can focus better. There's an anti-aging component. There are also benefits to skin care and muscle enhancement. That all helps with the symptoms that I have. After completing the initial four-session program, I will be going back every three months for a single treatment.

I've done extensive reading on the subject of brain recovery from stroke. In a nutshell, the brain is an energy-intensive organ that relies heavily on mitochondrial function for its activity. Reduced mitochondrial function is common among stroke patients. Several studies have shown that by replenishing NAD levels, mitochondrial function will improve. Perhaps that's why my hand and my overall body feel much better.

Cognitive improvement is also something I'm quite interested in and read a lot about. Some studies suggest that NAD therapy can improve cognitive function by accelerating the repair of damaged brain cells and tissue. In my case, improvement in my speech is something I've been striving for ever since the stroke back in 2015.

I'm always looking for ways to get better. So far, this one has proven to be quite productive.

———————

Regardless of how good helmets ever get, there is simply no way to completely remove the risk of concussions in the sport of ice hockey. Heck, there have been cases where a player's head wasn't struck and he still ended up with a brain injury after a violent collision simply because when the body was suddenly stopped, the brain had no braking system. It wanted to keep on moving until it hit something.

I definitely had at least one major concussion during my career, which was chronicled in the chapter about the incident with Chris Chelios at Montreal back in 1989. No two concussions are the same, and there are a crazy number of symptoms that go with them.

Keith Primeau arrived on the Flyers in 2000 in the Rod Brind'Amour trade with Carolina. Primeau, a big guy, didn't mind putting his body in harm's way and no doubt that made him a target. In a 2000 Game 6 playoff game against Pittsburgh, he was knocked cold by Penguins defenseman Bob Boughner. Primeau had to be taken to a Pittsburgh hospital, where he spent the night. This is just one of several concussions he suffered. The thing about concussions is you can experience nausea and other things that can affect your health. For me, it had a negative impact on my memory.

Having watched Primeau play, one could see that multiple concussions were catching up with him. After the Boughner hit, he had to retire a few years later because some of the lingering symptoms were affecting his everyday life. To his credit, some 20 years later he's still doing some commendable work with concussion people up in Canada. I know most of the people that are there. Here's something that will tell you how committed Keith is to concussion research: When he leaves this world, he promises he's leaving his brain to be used for medical research to help with finding better ways to treat this type of injury, including CTE (chronic traumatic encephalopathy). Now that's backing up your words with actions.

Keith has occasional trouble with some rather routine stuff, like driving a car. His wife has to go with him to make sure everything is OK.

Another towering player in our sport, Chris Pronger, also had to retire after getting struck directly in the face by an errant stick and suffering eye damage while he was playing for the Flyers at the Wells Fargo Center. He also had at least three other documented concussions. Pronger had some of the typical symptoms—nausea, trouble thinking—and his recovery was never quite complete. He had to retire somewhat prematurely at age 37 when he probably could have played past 40. Pronger suffered from dizziness, which I've never experienced, but it has to be awful.

Maybe the biggest, most powerful player to be the victim of concussions was Eric Lindros, who missed an entire season after he was wiped out in a check by New Jersey Devils defenseman Scott Stevens in Game 7 of the 2000 Stanley Cup Eastern Conference Final. There had been concussions before that hit and maybe more after. Like Primeau and Pronger, Lindros had to retire years before the age he was expected to call it quits.

Working against Lindros was his penchant for allowing his head to drop slightly and lower his sightline to follow the puck. This is a no-no in professional hockey. Lindros was so big at such an early age that he probably didn't have to worry about getting hit by kids who were six inches shorter. But when he got to the NHL, there were plenty of headhunters like Stevens and Pittsburgh's Darius Kasparaitis just waiting to pounce.

To his credit, Eric has followed Primeau's lead and works with the folks who do research up in Canada.

Concussions are tough on people and players are aware of the inherent risks that dog the sport. Some say the game isn't as violent as it once was, but when there is a high-speed collision nowadays with bigger, faster skaters than a generation or two ago, the fallout is worse.

One possible solution might be to expand the size of the rinks, possibly to something near the size of the playing surfaces in Europe. The Olympic-sized rinks are longer and wider than the 200-by-85-foot expanses used in the NHL. Of course, there are plenty of problems with that, like tearing out some seats in NHL buildings to accommodate the bigger rinks. That would be a costly logistical headache. The larger surfaces might cut down on the number of collisions because there is more room to skate. Then again, the North American game has created a style that has been around for a hundred years and switching over to something different might not go over too well with the hockey public.

Advances in helmet technology haven't done much to lower the concussion numbers either. Statistics show a player can receive a concussion without even a direct blow to the head. A violent blow to the body, in which there is a sudden stop, can cause the brain to rattle off the inside of the skull and still cause damage. How are they going to legislate hitting out of a game and not call it pond hockey?

I don't know if there's a connection between concussions and strokes, but I wouldn't bet against it.

————————

Back in the late 20th century, walking into some NHL locker rooms might give one the impression he was entering a professional horse racing stable.

That's because the use of the DMSO (dimethyl sulfoxide), a nonsteroidal antiflammatory agent given to draw fluid from the lungs of a horse with pulmonary edema or reduce swelling of the

spinal cord from a disease like West Nile virus, became so preva-
lent with ice hockey players. Allegedly it enhanced performance.

It worked for a lot of players. Only trouble was, it made change
rooms smell like barns. The smell was awful, and it took a long
time to get rid of that noxious odor.

Going back to the '80s, performance-enhancing drugs weren't
the problem. Drinking was. A good friend of mine, Flyers Hall of
Fame goaltender Bernie Parent, waged a battle with alcohol abuse
until about 1978. He knew he had a problem, even though he
won a couple Conn Smythe Trophy awards as Stanley Cup MVP
in 1973–74 and 1974–75. By '78, he decided to stop drinking,
and he continues to honor that pledge 45 years later. I talk with
him and he notices that sobriety makes a big difference for him.

With Paul Holmgren, he was a player, coach, and general
manager of the Flyers and later became general manager of the
old Hartford Whalers. He got into a bad car accident in March
of 1994 when he was drinking and driving and lost his license.
It was after a visit to the Betty Ford Clinic that he decided to
stop drinking.

I would venture to say that drinking was the biggest problem for professional hockey in the '80s and '90s. When you talk
about former Flyers defenseman Chris Therien, who recently co-
authored his autobiography *Road to Redemption*, he's gone through
some well-documented problems with drinking. He had to figure
it out. It took a long time. Now he helps the recovery community
through his work with rehab centers around Philadelphia. Another
ex-Flyer, Todd Fedoruk, had problems with alcohol, cocaine, and
painkillers. He's straightened out right now and serves as a game
analyst on Flyers radio broadcasts. John Kordic, the brother of
ex-Flyer Dan Kordic, died tragically of a drug overdose when he
was only 27 years old. And ex-Flyer Dave "the Hammer" Schultz
stopped drinking about a year ago. It was tough for him, but I

knew there are a lot of people pulling for him in his quest to get his life back on track.

When painkillers started becoming more available, several players apparently got hooked. One of the popular ones was oxycodone, which belong to a class of drugs known as opioid analgesics. It works in the brain to change how your body feels and responds to pain. Other painkillers that had big followings were Vicodin and codeine. These were sought after and caused a big problem because they were so addictive. I know one prominent ex-Flyer was caught on the U.S.-Canada border not too long ago with a stash of these types of drugs and was detained by law enforcement. There was some fallout from that incident.

From what I can gather, today's player doesn't drink as much as the guys back in the '80s and '90s. I know that when we played the Edmonton Oilers, there was a lot of talk that the Oilers were using cocaine. Testing wasn't as sophisticated in those days, so they could have gotten away with that.

For me, it was more about drinking beer. It was a good way to relax after a hard-fought game. I steered away from the drugs. In today's world, everything has changed. Marijuana is readily available, and a lot of states have made it legal. Substances like that can ease the pain from injuries caused by the naturally physical nature of the sport. In the '90s, when players started to make more money and were more financially solvent, a lot of them probably tried steroids. Especially defensemen, whose job it was to keep opposing forwards from getting to the net and who had to have the speed and weight to prevent that from happening. Anything to get a little stronger, a little faster. The forwards probably didn't need steroids as much because their job was to get from one place on the ice to the other as quickly as possible and they didn't need the extra bulk. Forwards have to be able to skate faster and be shifty on the attack.

There were times when I was thinking about something to ease the pain, including my somewhat serious eye injury and one or two concussions. I didn't feel like I needed painkillers, I just healed by myself without using anything else. The eye thing was very uncomfortable. I couldn't read a lot. I missed a total of eight games and then I was back at it.

In today's game there's a lot more money and players can afford to use stuff recreationally. But there seems to be a lot less of everything. Guys are so fit, they don't drink too much. They're faster; they have their own coaches and private chefs to prepare their food. It really makes a difference.

There's one other big difference between current times and those of the past: players today work out all year round. They might take off a week or two after the season ends, but then they get right back at it. Competition for jobs is so fierce at training camps that no one wants to get left behind. Plus, the science is so much more exact now. Everything is driven by computer analytics—from body fat to respiration rate. If a player has a fitness shortcoming, the training staff is going to find it.

Things were a lot different in the '80s. Players might do a little off-season running or lift a weight or two, but that was about it. If you needed to lose 10 pounds of beer weight for the regular season, you waited until the start of training camp, then went at it full bore. Everyone was in the same boat, so getting back in shape was kind of a group effort.

There are still some alcoholics out there, and occasionally you read about someone with an issue who gets suspended or winds up in a treatment program.

Personally, I haven't had a drink in more than eight years. After the stroke, it was time to say goodbye to that world because I knew alcohol was no longer good for me. To be perfectly honest, I don't miss it. I pride myself on being the designated driver. And

I have a boat. I let people drink on it and I don't. I can navigate the water without worrying about being impaired.

I don't miss drinking. When you first go dry, there might be a craving or two, but that begins to pass. Now I rarely even think about it.

CHAPTER 34

WORLDLY TASTES

I F YOU REALLY WANT TO get to know the real me, you have to learn about what really gets my juices going. And I can tell you this—I've been pretty much all over the world, a lot of the travel and living abroad connected to ice hockey. Be it food, beverage, ice rinks, you name it—I've got a list of tried-and-true favorites. I love to try new products and then go back for more.

Who knew that a kid from Saskatchewan would acquire such worldly tastes? Yet it made sense, because while hockey was quite time consuming, there was still time to experience new adventures, be they in France, Germany, Canada, or the United States.

One of the noteworthy ventures involved membership in a rather exclusive wine-tasting fraternity, the Chevaliers du Tastevin, which loosely translates to "Fraternity of Knights of the Wine-Tasters' Cup." There are 36 sections around the world with 12,000 members, and I was part of the Haddonfield, New Jersey, group for 10 years until I had my stroke in 2015. That's when I pretty much had to stop consuming alcohol.

The overall experience was special for me because the main type of wine was Burgundy from France only. When you do this, you tend to be a wine connoisseur. In general, they had events, maybe as many as four or five per year. There's a lot going around these wine-tasting get-togethers. Everyone gets dressed up. The meals are superb. In Haddonfield, there's plenty of world-class wine. I really loved the experience and learned a lot from it.

My interest in all this dates back to the end of my professional hockey career, which took place in France in the mid-'90s. I had a chance to travel all through France and that was both fun and educational. During those trips I had a chance to visit some wineries and get a real sense of how wine is produced. My favorite wine is a pinot noir.

Of course, what would a discussion about French wine be without mention of the famous Dom Pérignon champagne? When I was in France, I learned that Dom Pérignon was made by Moët & Chandon. It became special to me because I visited there. Their champagne is simply out of this world. Every plaudit it receives is well deserved. I really enjoyed getting to know the product.

Being in France for a year to play hockey, I had a chance to sample some of their other tasty beverages and food. There were things to get before a hockey game that tasted good but didn't sit too heavily in your stomach. We would stop at little cafés and pick up a cup of coffee and my favorite pregame food—a chocolate croissant. Acting as a player-coach for Anglet Hormadi Élite was certainly one of the fun times of my professional career, which was quickly winding down by 1995. When I was there, the baguettes were second to none, especially the ones in Paris. They had a little cheese and maybe a few other ingredients, which really made them special.

I got to know some of the members of the Chevaliers group and that was a great time.

Closer to home, I want to say a few words about cheesesteaks, which are one of Philadelphia's greatest claims to fame. But I'm here to tell you that one of the tastiest cheesesteaks I ever had was down at a place called Voltaco's at the Jersey Shore in Ocean City,

New Jersey. Man, they were good. In fact, those were probably the best cheesesteaks I've ever had. Unfortunately, they just recently closed, but in their day, they were at the very top of my list.

The best dinner I've ever had was at one of Philadelphia's most famous restaurants, Le Bec-Fin, another establishment that is no longer with us. The menu there was outstanding. I got very spoiled with that. Across town, the best steaks for my money are at Capital Grille. Get the 16-ounce filet mignon and you can't go wrong. Then top it off with some apple pie from Johnson's Corner Farm in Medford, New Jersey, with a little Midnight blend at Dunkin' Donuts. And one more—the best pasta sauce has to be Chef Vola's in Atlantic City. They must import this stuff from Sicily.

Now, when it comes to hockey, how can you beat the old Montreal Forum on a snowy Saturday night with all the fans cheering their lungs out? That's as pure as you're going to get. Enough Stanley Cup banners hanging from the rafters to fill the Hockey Hall of Fame. The ghosts of Maurice "Rocket" Richard, Guy Lafleur, and Jean Beliveau floating above the ice. Having grown up in Canada and dreamt about playing there, it was truly a fantasy come true. The Forum had the best ice because they only played games there, no practices or college games. On the flip side, I didn't particularly like going to Buffalo because the old Aud didn't have much atmosphere. I just didn't get along with that place.

Montreal was a great place to go out on the town. There were some excellent beers. They were almost as good as the ones in Germany, where I had time to do some taste-testing when I played there in the World Championships in 1983. The beer was just outstanding.

Let's not forget back home in Saskatchewan. I loved Labatt Blue from Saskatoon, the province's largest city. That went down real easy.

I have a place down in South Jersey, and so I'm partial to the sticky buns they serve at Mallon's in Ocean City. Just an amazing sugar high. When they're served hot, it's pure bliss.

Last but not least, if you're into vodka, try Fred Baxter's Plush Vodka from Moorestown, New Jersey. Here's to your health!

CHAPTER 35

FLYERS FANS

URING MY DECADE-PLUS CAREER with the Flyers, there was one aspect of the local game that always brought a smile to my face: the fans. And when I say fans, I mean it in the truest sense of the word—"fanatics." If there was a more intimidating place to play hockey than the old Spectrum in the '70s and '80s, I was never there. Some of it might have had something to do with the style of hockey played, à la the Broad Street Bullies. Also, the city of Philadelphia prides itself on being somewhat of a blue-collar town, and the Flyers' swashbuckling attitude fits right in with that personality.

The old barn at Broad and Pattison could downright scare some teams. An opposing player or two might contract a case of "Flyer Flu" and be a little nervous about playing such an imposing lineup. Plus you had the ear-rattling noise from the stands. Is it any wonder the Flyers once finished a 40-game home schedule with a record of 36–2–2 in the 1975–76 season?

Sign-making was also a budding art in the spectator sections, and no one displayed more wit than Dave "Sign Man" Leonardi. His first sign, created back in 1972, was a caricature of Don "Big Bird" Saleski. Dave, who sat directly behind the opponent's net for two of the three periods, once said he realized he could reach more people with the written word rather than just yelling stuff.

He held up big, clever signs, and almost the whole building just had to look.

Once original radio broadcaster Gene Hart noticed one of the signs and mentioned it over the air, Leonardi's work really took off. As the Bullies caught on, the signs grew in number. There were ones like "Rick the Quick" for Rick MacLeish or "Kelly Power" for Bob Kelly—or if an opposing netminder was having a tough time, it was "Next Goalie." His favorites are "Start the Bus" and "Shake Hands & Leave."

Flyers fans are about as passionate as they come. They make the trek from central Pennsylvania or southern Delaware or all parts of New Jersey to watch the games and cheer on their favorite players. The passion was really born in the Stanley Cup seasons, when seemingly every sports fan in Philadelphia jumped on board the bandwagon. The fervor really didn't slow down much in the '80s as we went to the Stanley Cup Final three times. The fans wholeheartedly embraced us.

The Flyers Fan Club has been around since the inception of the team in 1967. The thing about the fan club is they are enthusiastic when the Flyers win, and they are enthusiastic when the Flyers don't win. It's not a fair-weather fraternity. First, they have monthly meetings during the season. At their first meeting, they invite a new player to join in, say a few words, and discuss what's it like to have the support of the city and their loyal fans. The club also takes part in several road trips, and it's always nice to see fans wearing friendly Flyers jerseys in hotel lobbies and down by the glass holding signs before the game starts. In addition, the club helps out with charitable events such as the Gritty 5K and the Flyers Charities Carnival. Finally, the club has group outings during and after the season with offerings including a fantasy league, ticket opportunities, a newsletter, and a membership gift.

The club has expressed appreciation to meet new, young players who will play a part in the team's future. When Daniel Brière assumed the position of general manager in the summer of 2023, he made it a point to say the Flyers were fully engaged in a rebuild and that's why so much is riding on the play of young up-and-comers such as Bobby Brink, Tyson Foerster, Egor Zamula, and goaltender Samuel Ersson. Those are the players fan club members want to meet.

Flyers fans are known for their loyalty when it comes to getting autographs of and photographs with their favorite players. They will stand for hours in heat, rain, or snow in the parking lot at the Flyers Training Center in Voorhees, New Jersey, and that's a rather impressive sight. When they aren't outside, they're inside carefully watching practice to see which players are really into it. In training camp, if there's an intrasquad scrimmage (such as Team Clarke vs. Team Lindros), better get there early because by the opening whistle there won't be a seat to be found.

To me, a kid from rural Canada, it was eye-opening when I first deplaned in Philadelphia. I know the folks back home love hockey, but the fans who bleed Orange, Black, and White are right up there with them. I've been around here for 44 years, so it's safe to say I'm often recognized in public. I just smile and say hi, and that's about all I need to do.

For me, that Game 6 in 1987 stands out above all the rest when it comes to crowd noise. After I scored that goal to tie the game and then J.J. Daigneault got the winner, you couldn't hear yourself think. It was like a cross between a rock concert and walking to a private jet on the tarmac. That was awesome.

After my stroke, I lost some of the strength and coordination in my right hand, which I used to use to sign autographs for fans. I basically had to learn how to use my left hand for that skill. But it's easy because I'm somewhat ambidextrous and can do stuff with either hand. I worked on it a bit and now my signature looks pretty good, if I do say so myself.

———————

Anytime a small-town boy hits the big city, it's a bit of an eye-opener. So you can imagine what it was like for me coming from a town out on the Saskatchewan plains called Neudorf to a giant metropolis like Philadelphia. Welcome to the big city.

It's safe to say many professional athletes don't mind the hustle and bustle of the City of Brotherly Love. As a matter of fact, some, like me, look forward to it. There's something for everyone, be it historic buildings and statues, great places to eat, or plenty of spacious parks.

Personally, even though I'm from Canada, I have a certain fascination with United States history, especially as it pertains to the American Revolution and its aftermath. There's Independence Hall, where the Declaration of Independence was signed, as well as the Liberty Bell, which is about as symbolic of freedom as you can get in this country. Many Philadelphians have a special place in their hearts for the statue of William "Billy" Penn, which sits atop City Hall—you know; Penn as in Penn-sylvania. Loosely translated, it means Penn's Woods. For a long time, no buildings in Philadelphia were allowed to exceed the height of the Penn Statue.

If you're into boats like I am, you can head over to Boathouse Row, situated on East River Drive along the Schuylkill River, which is a sight to see when the sun goes down and the lights go on, reflecting off the water. Nearby is the Philadelphia Museum of Art, home to the works of some of the most famous artists in the world. A side trip to the Rodin Museum is worth the time and money. When you head downtown, a can't-miss stop is the

Union League, one of the most famous landmarks in the city. Their restaurant, the 1862, has to be one of the best in the city.

Not a day goes by that the good folks in this country don't get a glimpse of the Stars and Stripes. They can thank famous seamstress Betsy Ross for that. The Betsy Ross House is where it all happened. There were just 13 states on the original flag. She probably never could have imagined there would one day be 50.

At the top of the Pyramid Club downtown you can see to the horizon in just about every direction. From 50 stories up you can get a good look at Fairmount Park, which is where a lot of people go for some recreation or to just relax and take in the view.

You can't stop in Philadelphia without visiting two of the most famous cheesesteak joints in the world, Geno's and Pat's. The rivalry between the two establishments is almost as emotional as the one between the Hatfields and the McCoys—or the Flyers and Rangers, for that matter. These folks know how to put a meat sandwich together. The cool thing is you can watch them make one. When they're done, be sure to add some peppers to get your juices flowing. I believe each place has sold this wonderful concoction by the millions. You can order their specialties any way you want, which I think is one of the main reasons why they're so popular. I believe even a few out-of-town hockey players have stopped at these joints just to see if they're all they are cracked up to be.

When it comes to junk food, you won't find anything better than the French fries at a place called Chickie & Pete's. I don't know what they put in those things, but man are they tasty.

Now that there's a Chickie & Pete's just a few blocks from the Wells Fargo Center, it's a convenient place for hockey fans, scribes, and the like to stop in for a quick post-game burger and brew. The TV sets are still chirping with the games from the United States and Canada western metro centers. The talk at the tables is lively. When the topics turn to hockey, it's all about backing up your side of the debate with facts or strong opinions.

On a side note, for the past few years, the Flyers have hosted various teams from area high schools and the like to play at the Wells Fargo Center after NHL play has completed for the night. It's quite a thrill for these young players to compete on this special ice surface, even if you only happen to have a handful of family members in a 19,000-seat arena on hand to watch the proceedings. Chances are, if it's not a school night, some of them might just end up at Chickie & Pete's to review what just took place on the WFC ice.

Lots of cities have bad traffic problems, but Philadelphia is lucky to have a big highway, Interstate 95, running north/south, plus a good crosstown carrier, the Vine Street Expressway. If you have a sense of where you're going, it's not all that difficult to figure out.

Now, if you're into gambling, Philadelphia has become a popular drawing card for that sort of thing. No need to drive all the way to Atlantic City or fly out to Vegas. There's the "Live!" casino just a few blocks away from where the Flyers play at the Wells Fargo Center. If someone's had one too many, there are plenty of hotel rooms right on site. Just up the road resides the Rivers Casino and a little north of that Parx Casino. If you don't mind driving a little farther, there's Valley Forge Casino, about a half hour out of town.

Let me just say a few words about the fans in Philadelphia. They have a reputation for being passionate—perhaps a little too boisterous at times. For me, they've been awesome. Now, it's true we were in the playoffs every year in the '80s, and that made for a lot of fair-weather fans. But even in the down years, like 1990–94, the fans came out in great numbers to support the Flyers and their players.

The fans in this town want their money's worth. They expect a player to be a hard worker and give an honest effort and if they don't, they're going to hear about it. As mentioned, most of the players love to play in Philadelphia. They would rather the fans be overly passionate than just sit there in their seats not making any noise. Maybe that's why the Flyers have always gone in big on character players—the guys who wear their hearts on their sleeves and their knuckles in someone else's face. That's why a guy like Dave Schultz was just as popular as someone like Hall of Famer Bob Clarke.

If you don't have character players in Philadelphia, the fans are going to know right away and it's not going to work. You might have all the skills in the world, but if you don't have guys who are willing to lay it on the line, you won't be feeling any passion from the stands.

The bottom line is this: You need skill to win games, but you also need those character guys to win over the faithful. That's why I was encouraged when I learned Keith Jones and Daniel Brière had been hired as president of hockey operations and general manager, respectively. All they talk about is reconnecting with the fans, a bridge that was lost for a while after the passing of team founder and co-owner Ed Snider a few years back. The "New Era of Orange" is a step in the right direction.

For a building that was constructed in about a year's time, the Spectrum in Philadelphia sure had a lot to offer. Completed in time for the Flyers' first season, 1967–68, the first thing that struck you about the place was its intimacy. Even the cheap seats upstairs seemed to be much closer to the ice surface than in other buildings.

Hockey was somewhat of a novelty in Philadelphia, so the team was bound to draw big crowds whether it experienced a decent season on the ice or not. The Spectrum's completion only added to the excitement. First, you had the iconic Flyers logo at center ice. The "P" with the puck in the middle and the wings on the back made for a sleek design. In my opinion, it's one of the best of all time. It's a symbol of what the Flyers are all about.

Folks on the second level could get into the game because the angles afforded great views of the action. Fans in Philly are loud to begin with, and the acoustics in the building at Broad and Pattison only made it seem that much noisier. It became an intimidating place to play, especially when the Flyers started loading up with guys like Schultz, Don "Big Bird" Saleski, André "Moose" Dupont, and others. They became known as the Broad Street Bullies, and soon there were reports of a few opposing players wanting to sit out games in South Philadelphia. The formula seemed to work. The nastier the Flyers got, the more they seemed to win.

In a rather twisted way, the whole thing gave the Flyers what you might call character or an identity. That might be something the Flyers have lacked in recent years. But bringing on board heavyweights such as Nick Deslauriers might be reversing that trend. Occasionally the Wells Fargo Center sounds a bit like the old Spectrum, but there probably hasn't been enough physical play to the fans' liking. You won't find too many Flyers fans who don't want the team to resemble that rowdy bunch back in the '70s, when there were fights and hard hits galore. That's all you need to know about how intimidating the place was.

Ironically, the 1975 Flyers had the last All-Canadian roster to win the Stanley Cup—not a single American or European to be found. Granted, much of the NHL was composed of Canadian players in that era, but usually you had one or two players from outside maple leaf country. When you have all the players talking with the same accent, it adds an extra element of closeness.

One of the most iconic moments at the old barn was the start of the tradition of having popular singer Kate Smith perform "God Bless America" before Stanley Cup playoff games. Nowhere was this more prominent than before Game 6 of the 1974 Stanley Cup Final. Kate was standing at center ice with the spotlight beaming down on her when the Bruins' Bobby Orr came skating over to present her with a bouquet of flowers. It didn't matter. The Flyers won the game and the championship anyway.

I really liked playing at the Spectrum because the rink and the action were close to the fans. It had charm, and there wasn't a dry eye to be found when they finally decided to knock the place down in 2008–09.

It didn't take a sociologist to figure out why no one was moving back north of the border when their career ended. Many from that outfit decided to live and work in the Philadelphia area. You had the friendship and business connections, but you also had the famous Jersey Shore, which was a big attraction to guys who grew up in the chilly north. It was only a little over an hour away from where we played games and practiced. Nowadays, when guys come into money, they buy a second home down by the ocean. It's a great place to spend the summer months.

As for staying in the Philadelphia area, the money side of it was nice, but the friendship connections I made during my playing days were just as important. I planned on staying, even while I was playing for the Flyers. What was I going to do? Go home to Canada and work on a farm? Too much had happened since I left home at an early age, and living in the United States was the only real option. I gave it a lot of thought. It was nice that I had played hockey here in the States for 15 years. I had gotten accustomed to the lifestyle. I felt comfortable with the business connections

I had already made during my playing career, so the decision to stay here was probably made for me. So I decided to finally not think about returning to some of those minus-40-degree nights north of the border.

If a professional hockey player doesn't want to be playing and living under the bright lights, he might as well cross Philadelphia off his destination list. This isn't a one-newspaper town, although the media covering the team has shrunk a bit in recent years. I'm guessing the changing economy has something to do with that. Still, the stars in any sport burn brightly here in the nation's sixth-largest city. The Eagles, Phillies, and Sixers have been serious contenders in recent years, and the Flyers want to get back into that elite fraternity.

Back in the last century before some of today's modern technology, the internet was just getting a foot in the door. A lot of the media stuff was old school. Maybe the player-writer relationships were a bit closer. Trust might be the key word. If a player was asked to speak off the record for information purposes, that dialogue was kept private, and sources were protected. Somewhere along the line that agreement began to fall apart.

Don't think for a minute a vast majority of players don't read their press clippings. In fact, if a player is too thrifty to purchase a newspaper either at a newsstand or online in these modern times, there's often some sort of clip service provided by teams to keep their players informed.

Hockey is such a fast-paced, exciting game that scribes tend to get caught up in all the hubbub at times. Their job is to analyze a team's performance, maybe even play coach every so often and even second-guess the guy standing behind the bench.

Now, if a writer criticizes a particular player a little too frequently, he could wind up in a heated confrontation. If you play the game long enough, you're going to see a player poking his finger an inch or two away from a writer's nose or sometimes something much worse than that. But at the end of the day, hockey writers are no different than restaurant or Broadway show evaluators. Their assignment is to critique the product, good or bad, and occasionally someone's feathers do get ruffled.

The Philadelphia Inquirer and the *Daily News* pretty much covered the team on a daily basis. That went all the way back to the days of the old *Philadelphia Bulletin*. Sportswriter Jack Chevalier was credited with coming up with the term "Broad Street Bullies" in the early '70s. Other suburban papers, such as the *Camden (N.J.) Courier-Post*, the *Delaware County Daily Times*, and the *Bucks County Courier Times*, provided comprehensive coverage as well.

Individual players began to learn which writers they could trust and open up to. Most reporters were fair with their coverage. Hockey was the new kid in town—it had been there for only a little over a decade when I arrived—and with all their early success, the Flyers had a lot of favorable stories written about them.

It was a pretty good setup for both sides. Media members could wander around the dressing room and begin a conversation with just about any player they wanted. Again, if the reporter provided fair coverage over a period of time, he would gain trust. Guys would sit by their lockers after games, and you could talk to them. Now it's a little different after games. A short list of names is drawn up and those are the only guys who are going to talk unless special accommodations are made. At least that allows the other players to ride the bike or wind down after a charged-up, emotional game. It's rather different than my playing days, to say the least.

The media in all four cities I played in treated me really well. I guess some of that had to do with the fact that nearly every place I played we won a lot more than we lost. Five trips to the Stanley Cup Final without a win might be frustrating to some, but I view it as a unique accomplishment.

I was always thinking about things to talk about. Going on and on about checking schemes and power plays can get a little tedious at times. Some players just had a knack for saying the right thing, maybe interjecting a little humor or an observation here or there. The Flyers were certainly not at a loss for interesting topics. Some of the comments are funny. Most of the young guys really don't know how to brand themselves. They answer questions generically with more than a bit of caution, like I did in my first couple years. The last thing I needed was something controversial coming out of my mouth. So I didn't say much for that very reason.

Whether it was the *Boston Globe* or the *Star Tribune*, I always felt like I got a fair shake. Plus, all the teams I played for seemed to have good leaders who served as spokespersons. When you have excellent quote machines like Rick Tocchet, Ray Bourque, or Bobby Smith, you can just sort of sit off to the side and listen. They communicated really well.

As for the coaches, they did what they could to protect their players. If anyone was going to criticize a player or two, the coach felt it was his job, not some guy's from a newspaper. Every once in a while a reporter would be critical, and a coach would have to repel that attack. Maybe later he would address the issue with the player in private.

It's much easier to deal with the media when you're successful. The public likes to jump on the bandwagon when you're doing well, and the media senses that and usually jumps onboard. In my 10 full seasons in Philadelphia, we never had a losing record.

There was similar success in Boston and Minnesota, so I seldom felt the critical light being shined on me. We had good teams and never "got in trouble." At the end of the day, almost everything written or broadcast about me seemed fair.

CHAPTER 36

POST-CAREER PLANS

WHILE A PLAYER MIGHT THINK it takes seemingly forever to somehow get to the National Hockey League, the usual stay at the top isn't. Statistics show the average player only lasts about five years or so in the big show and only some of the elite or better-trained athletes make it past their 30th birthday. Just look at most of today's NHL rosters. A lot of them were born in the 21st century, and that's a rather eye-opening number.

That's why it's so important for professional hockey players to plan ahead. Chances are they will not make enough money to simply retire, fly off to some faraway beach, and sip Mai Tais for the rest of their lives. Besides, that would be boring.

A small percentage will stay in the game in some fashion, be it coaching, general managing, scouting, or broadcasting. Most of the rest will have to find gainful employment elsewhere. There have been countless stories of players who didn't think about their futures during their playing careers and when the grim reaper (aka, pink slip) finally did arrive, they didn't have a clue what to do next.

I was fortunate enough to find several undertakings to my liking. I started with hockey rink construction, wound up in the radio broadcast booth at Flyers games for the better part of a decade, and then transferred into several other fields, including real estate sales. I took business classes as well to learn what I could. Plus, charity work has filled a lot of my time and that never gets old. All those things add up when you need to change your career to something besides hockey.

Dave Poulin and I played at the same time in our careers, first with the Flyers and later with Boston. Dave did his under-graduate work at the University of Notre Dame and maintained his connections there during his playing career. That's why it was a smooth connection back to the Fighting Irish when his NHL career finally ended. He started out by coaching at the school in South Bend, Indiana, for 10 years. That was followed by a two-year stint in a search firm. From there he joined the Toronto Maple Leafs' management team. In recent years, he's created his own radio/TV show in Toronto and continues to be successful.

As for preparing for the final curtain in the NHL, there are lots of good options that get you ready. Three ex-Flyers, goal-tender Brian Elliott and forwards James van Riemsdyk and Sam Gagner, have taken advantage of the National Hockey League Players' Association's athlete development program in association with Harvard University Business School, which is tailored to athletes.

Those three have already utilized the knowledge they've gained in preparation for life off the ice. Elliott recently retired, but Gagner and van Riemsdyk keep chugging along although both are in their mid-thirties and know they haven't got much time left in pro hockey.

The program is designed to equip athletes with the tools required to be successful in business. It matches athletes with a pair of Harvard Business School MBA student mentors, who work with the athletes to help develop their business acumen to make sound business decisions.

JVR has praised the program, saying it was an approachable one. The Flyers' former first-round draft pick (No. 2 overall) in 2007 was selected while he played and studied at the University of New Hampshire. The Flyers wanted him to join them the same year he was drafted, but James and his family requested he stay at UNH for another year, which he did.

Elliott always came across to me as a thinking man's goaltender. One professor said players like Elliott and Gagner could easily make the transition into the Harvard MBA program.

Back in the greater Philadelphia area, former Flyers star Tim Kerr has made a name for himself in a second career in real estate sales in South Jersey. Even during his playing career, he was always involved in other things, like an automobile dealership. Then he started a restaurant down at the Jersey Shore, which became very popular. Now he's a realtor in Avalon, New Jersey, and having been a Flyers mainstay for so many years certainly hasn't hurt his name recognition when it comes to sales. His two sons, Garret and Wesley, work with him.

The bottom line is this—no matter how long one plays in professional hockey, it's always smart to have a backup plan for a rainy day. And you can never start too early making one.

CHAPTER 37

ASK NOT FOR WHOM
THE BELL TOLLS

SOMETIMES THE LAST PERSON in the hockey world to know it's time for you to retire is…you. Maybe your numbers are still acceptable and your overall game is still good enough to get you by, but there are going to be a couple times in a match when you realize you have become a step slow, either in your legs or in your thinking process. It's just a fact; as you age, the reflexes slowly decline, and the reaction time just isn't as fast as it used to be. You still want to compete at a high level, but the body doesn't always want to cooperate.

That was pretty much the case for me. By 1993 I was at a crossroads. After a couple years with the old Minnesota North Stars, there was no automatic contract renewal coming. The stark reality was I was a free agent for really only the second time in my career. I was well into my thirties and, while my production was beginning to drop, I still wanted to reach those 1,000-game, 1,000-point markers. If I wanted to squeeze out another season, I knew I was going to have to make some concessions, like possibly a utility role on a fourth line.

As it turns out, I was fortunate enough to hook up with the old Hartford Whalers for what figured to be a final season. So

I wasn't really blindsided by this predetermination. As soon as I got to four figures, it was going to be a year in France for what amounted to some fun and games. But playing a sport for so many years, I wanted to make sure I achieved the goals I had set many years back.

Today, most contracts are structured on a routine three-year cycle. Sometimes the better players get more years (and more money), mainly because they are key components to their teams. Considering the average NHL career only lasts about five years, the end of the line can come a lot quicker than most players might hope. But they all want to hang on as long as they can because the contracts have become so lucrative. Even with the salary cap, general managers can find ways to get creative. For some players, it's like payback for being a bit underpaid over the years.

Potential retirement has to do with a lot more than just money. When players leave the game, they know they're going to miss the lifestyle—the high of super-competitive games, the travel, the friendships they've developed. Just the excitement of being an NHL player and having the sports world pay homage to your talent is something one never forgets. There's a certain sense that you are playing with and against the very best and that this somehow validates your membership in a rather elite fraternity. That realization comes into sharper focus once you leave the game for good.

When a player gets older and is considering retirement, sometimes someone has to tell them that either the end is near or the end is here. Basically, I had to audition for a spot on the Whalers' roster. When you've been on a line with Gretzky and Lemieux in an international tournament, trying to earn a contract on an NHL team like the Whalers can be a somewhat humbling experience. Your ego kind of has to go out the window. I didn't know if I was going to be making the team or not and the uncertainty can keep you awake at night. At that point, I pretty much knew the end was coming. You might still have the will in your heart, but ultimately your mind is the rational party in that situation. That and finding out it takes a little longer to get out of bed the morning after a game the night before.

CHAPTER 38

THE FUTURE IS BRIGHT

THE MEMORIES OF THAT MORNING in late summer 2015 will be etched in my mind forever. I was once one of the best hockey players in the world and now, because of a stroke, I had been reduced to what might be described as a shell of myself. Even early on, I knew that the road back to some semblance of myself would be a long and arduous one.

By the time I was back at Magee Rehab in Philadelphia, I was still being transported around by a wheelchair to negate the risk of falling and striking my head. It was humbling, to say the least. Yet through all of this, I never let myself get down. I was determined to stay positive. It seemed like at least one member of my family was with me all the time. Friends like Scott McKay stopped by all the time to offer words of encouragement. Guys I had known since my young adulthood, like Ray Allison, were a steady presence.

From my connections to the business world, the guys from the Judge Group, I knew a lot of them, including Marty Judge. They called me all the time to see how I was doing and wishing me the best.

By this time, Ed Snider was starting to show signs of failing health of his own (he passed away in April 2016). Mr. Snider helped me financially while I wasn't working during my medical leave. It made a difference to help pay my bills, especially the medical stuff, which was pretty expensive each month.

I started each day with a prayer. I was thankful God was with me. Being an athlete, daily routine was important. When you have that as your support structure, it seems to help the healing process. During my playing career I suffered some significant injuries. The eye injury cost me eight games, but don't be fooled by the brevity of the forced absence. It was serious enough to almost end my career. The knee and hand injuries were pretty significant as well.

Through it all I was determined to remain positive and not give in to doubt or remorse. Faith, family, friends, and Flyers alumni really helped me get through when the stroke happened.

I kept the faith. I learned from my dad, the Lutheran minister, that you should treat all people the same way. My dad always said if you believe in Jesus Christ with your heart that you will be saved after you die on Earth. I always remembered that and kept that close to my beliefs.

Connecting with fellow stroke survivors has really enriched my life because it makes you realize you're not alone in your struggle to survive. They talk with me, give me advice, and provide companionship.

One guy, John Cooper, almost died due to a brain injury. He wrote a book and he's one of the guys I speak with at least once a month. He's shown much improvement, sort of on the same timeline as me. Then there's Nick Avgousti—we skate in the morning at Pennsauken. He had a massive stroke approximately five years ago and almost died. Guys like John and Nick always have something supportive to say. They ask how you're doing. They know I'm busy setting up golf tournaments and other charity events. They say they want to support me any way they can, and that's always nice to hear.

Another fellow, Eric Toppy, almost died in a car crash a few years ago. He just came back from that, and he helped me set up a hockey charity event in New Jersey. We had a couple Flyers and Devils alumni playing in that.

These are examples of people I've met who understand how difficult the journey is to recovery. Reny Burckhardt lives near Ramblewood Golf Club in Mount Laurel, New Jersey. I get to talk with him a lot.

Former New York Rangers forward Brian Mullen had a stroke. I was at a Ronald McDonald golf tournament with him at Baltusrol Golf Club in Springfield, New Jersey. We recovered together along the same timeline, and he's given me praise for the improvements I've made. Another former hockey player, ex-Devils defenseman Ken Daneyko, has had a series of mini strokes. He's on TV now, and during my time on Flyers radio we talked a lot.

One of the guys I worked with at Bancroft, Kevin Sullivan, has helped me with charity events.

For people who have suffered strokes, I always talk about the "BEFAST" guidelines for recovery. B is for balance, which is so important in moving about. E is for eyes. If your vision is blurry, contact a physician. Same with F for face—if you see your face drooping, that's a warning sign. A is for arms. If your arms feel weak, that could be another telltale sign of a stroke. S is for speech. If the words come out slurred, again, it might be time to dial up a doctor. T is for time. If you suspect something is wrong, immediately dial 9-1-1.

A lot of people I know waited too long and didn't call for help right away. Getting medical attention right away can make a big difference. Every three minutes, someone in the U.S. dies of a stroke. Almost 800,000 Americans each year suffer a stroke.

Back in 2015, as my recovery from the stroke progressed and I finally had some of my ability to talk again, I set up a Zoom call with my family in Saskatchewan. By this time, my dad had slowed quite a bit due to dementia. But he was able to convey some ideas to me and one of them was that I was here for a higher purpose. That always stuck with me.

I haven't seen my grandchildren yet. Hopefully that will happen someday when I'm still around. I have some great stories to tell, especially the one about that angel on my wing.